# FUNDAMENTALIST FAVORITISM:

## The Biblical Discriminations

W. Wiebe

Note for Librarians: A cataloguing record for this book is available from Library and Archives Canada at www.collectionscanada.ca/amicus/index-e.html
ISBN 1-4120-9759-2

*Offices in Canada, USA, Ireland and UK*

**Book sales for North America and international:**
Trafford Publishing, 6E–2333 Government St.,
Victoria, BC V8T 4P4 CANADA
phone 250 383 6864 (toll-free 1 888 232 4444)
fax 250 383 6804; email to orders@trafford.com
**Book sales in Europe:**
Trafford Publishing (UK) Limited, 9 Park End Street, 2nd Floor
Oxford, UK OX1 1HH UNITED KINGDOM
phone +44 (0)1865 722 113 (local rate 0845 230 9601)
facsimile +44 (0)1865 722 868; info.uk@trafford.com
**Order online at:**
trafford.com/06-1515

10 9 8 7 6 5 4 3 2

INTRODUCTION

This book is <u>not</u> intended for those who view the Bible as an insignificant book. An Anglican Bishop was asked if he took the Bible literally. He responded that he didn't even take it seriously. This book is <u>not</u> for him.

This book is for people that have taken an interest in books like <u>The Purpose Driven Life</u> by R. Warren, who were left with the question: "Is Christianity really that simple and problem free?" Did it leave you feeling like a jury member after the defense has eloquently argued that black is white?

Bible School students will need this book for their term paper preparation and for their discussion groups.

Bible scholars will love this book for its concise re-evaluation of our Current Christian theologies in the light of the contents of the Bible.

This book requires of its readers that they possess a level of faith maturity that allows a closer analysis, that allows us to recognize unresolved problems without effecting a faith or emotional crisis.

It will appeal to those with a commitment to the continuing emancipation of all mankind. It is good that slavery has substantially ended. It will be good when continuing Christian discriminations cease.

Finally, this book is for those believers that rate themselves both intelligent and courageous. Intelligent because they know themselves capable of reading, studying and understanding. They have no need for intermediaries to tell them what the Bible and the "true faith" are all about. Courageous because the quest they have undertaken places the burden of determining their own right path on their own shoulders. The comfortable escape route is blocked for them: "I did and believed what my leader told me to." Courageous also because we will find difficult conundrums that the pablum and baby mash from most pulpits and books will never mention.

Go ahead! You have both intelligence and courage in full measure. It will be an exciting read.

Finally, it is well known that the Bible includes within its pages favoritism, famine, disease, murders, rapes, massacres and annihilations. By present United Nations standards it includes crimes against humanity, genocide and war crimes. It proceeds to the crucifixion and the seven bowls of God's wrath. It concludes with the final, eternal, side by side steady state of heavenly bliss for the saved few and hellish torture for the damned many. Thus it is not a "nice" book in the normal issues averse public mind. I may then be forgiven if this book, <u>Biblical Discriminations</u>, in dealing with these topics, may also be regarded as not "nice".

TABLE OF CONTENTS

# Chapter 1
# Gender Discrimination: Males Preferred

**Males Preferred?**

The last century has been a very tumultuous period with respect to gender discrimination in the western world. We are aware of the status of women prior to this period of rapid change. Women were helpless, non-thinking, career limited, non-voting, subservient, substandard humans. Great progress has been made. In many ways women are now the full equals of men, and where this equality is not fully implemented, laws and employer-employee contracts have been enacted to bring about the desired objective: gender equality. At this point it is fair to say that in the western world the majority opinion would hold that the gender discrimination of past centuries is a sordid and evil part of our history. We are gladly moving forward to a time when gender discrimination is fully overcome.

We are not there just yet. Huge implacable barriers have been in place and are yet in place to prevent full gender equality. Old-boys networks still do exist. Traditions still hold sway. And churches are reluctant to find fault with the patriarchal social ordering found both in the church and in the Bible. This reluctance is directly related to the church's commitment to stability, unchanging tradition and the sanctity, truth, utility and relevance of its foundation book, the Bible. Thus, the churches have been reluctant to probe into the question of biblical gender discrimination for fear of what they may find.

We will have no such fear. We will undertake the study, through the Bible, to answer this question in an academically thorough manner. The purpose will not be to strengthen or diminish faith. It will not be to bolster or weaken any Christian theology. It will be, however, to analyze and understand the writers of the Bible. This purpose will be accomplished by a journey through the Bible taking special note of those stories, directives and observations that bear on the status of women in relation to the status of men.

We will have to choose a particular Bible (or a set of Bibles) to journey through. We are aware that there are many translations from the original texts, and further that they do not always agree. It is my opinion that the disagreements tend to be minor, as long as one avoids the more radical, recent "tidied up" or gender neutral editions. The Bibles we will journey through are:

1. The New English Bible, with the Apocrypha.
   Oxford University Press, 1970.
2. The New American Bible, Catholic Biblical Association of
   America.St. Anthony Guild Press Patterson, New Jersey, 1970.

3. Bible for Today's Family, American Bible Society, New York, 1970.
4. The New Jerusalem Bible, Readers Edition, New York, 1990.
5. Holy Bible KJV Amplified, Parallel Bible, Zondervan Corporation, Grand Rapids, Michigan, 1987.
6. The Book. Tyndale House Publishers, Wheaton Illinois, 1984.

The Bible begins with Genesis, an account of the beginning or origin. In chapter two God creates Adam and places him in the Garden of Eden. At its centre are two trees, the tree of life and the tree of knowledge of good and evil. The latter he is forbidden to eat from; clearly it was permissible for him to eat from the tree of life. After creating animals and birds, God created Eve, making a partner (helper) suitable for him. Both Adam and Eve are still mortals having taken no interest in the tree of life and are still functioning as amoral beings having no knowledge of good and evil. The serpent arrives. Eve reminds the serpent that we may eat of all trees except the tree of knowledge of good and evil, lest you die. The serpent countered "of course you will not die. God knows that as soon as you eat from it, your eyes will be opened and you will be like the gods knowing both good and evil." She took and she ate. She gave some to Adam, he also ate. The serpent was right: they did not die, their eyes were opened, but instead of a sudden realization that they had committed an evil disobedience to God, they realized with instant shame that they were naked. Further, they retained their mortal status, because God now decided to deny any access to the tree of life by driving them out of the Garden of Eden.

The punishment was indeed heavy. Neither Eve nor Adam was even slightly aware at the time when they ate the forbidden fruit that their act of disobedience was good or evil. Unsettling questions about God arise immediately:

1) Why not create Adam and Eve already endowed with the god-like wisdom of the knowledge of good and evil?

2) If God preferred the original amoral status of Adam and Eve, why put the forbidden tree in the garden?

3) Does not mankind owe Eve a debt of gratitude for gaining for us this god-like wisdom of good and evil, which clearly God wished to deny us?

4) Does the serpent not play a positive role in the enhancement of the genuine wisdom of mankind? Would we have gained this god-like wisdom without the intervention of Satan in his serpent disguise?

In addition to these unsettling questions, we see that the door to punishment by God had been opened and punishment was rained down.

The serpent became more accursed than all other animals; it was forced to crawl on its belly and "dust shall you eat all the days of your life." This curse reflects the lack of any skill or expertise in animal behavior observation. Snakes do not eat dust. Go to any zoo and ask them what snakes eat. This fact was so embarrassing to the writers of the The Book that their pen transcribes "you shall eat dust" into "you shall grovel in the dust". [The Book. Genesis 3:14]

Next came Eve. If ever punishment was inordinately heavy, this was the time. She was hit with three curses:

Curse #1. Childbearing will be made intensely painful: "I will greatly multiply your grief and your suffering in the pregnancy and the pangs of childbearing; with spasms of distress you will bring forth children". [KJV Amplified Holy Bible. Genesis 3:16]

Curse #2. "You shall be eager for your husband" [New English Bible. Genesis 3:16] OR "yet your desire and craving shall be for your husband" [KJV Amplified Holy Bible. Genesis 3:16] OR "your urge shall be for your husband" [New American Bible. Genesis 3: 16]

Curse #3 "And he will rule over you" [KJV Amplified Holy Bible.Genesis 3:16] OR "And he shall be your master" [New American Bible. Genesis 3:16] OR "And he will dominate you" [New Jerusalem Bible. Genesis 3:16]

Finally it is Adam's turn. His punishment begins with the words "Because you listened to your wife" and continues. The ground you till will be cursed yielding up food only by the sweat of your brow, constantly overpowered by weeds, specifically thorns and thistles. Curiously, perhaps as a precursor to God's rejection of Cain's "offering to the Lord from the fruit of the soil" [New American Bible. Genesis 4:3] this relatively mild punishment seems aimed exclusively at tillers of the soil and certainly less so at the keepers of flocks.

Let us review the curses put in place by God against all women (Eve). Child bearing will be a painful process. Indeed the curse seems to overlook the fact that child bearing often goes beyond painful, it becomes fatal. Any visit to an older cemetery reveals the countless names of younger women who died of one or more of the many complications resulting from pregnancy and childbirth. When painkilling drugs were introduced to reduce the intense pangs of childbirth, the churches objected saying it was very sinful to attempt in any way to escape, to skirt around, to invalidate Eve's curse. The objections stopped when Queen Victoria of England opted for drug induced pain reduction for her delivery.

The second curse was much worse. Eve was cursed with eagerness, urges, desires, and cravings for her husband. We have a picture then of the result of the curse being a woman driven by strong sexual urges. No such similar curse was put in place against men. Where ever sexual misconduct was to happen in the future, a wily, cunning, sexually driven woman was assumed to be the cause. Consider the following excerpt where the urges and desires of a married woman overpower her when her husband is gone.

"From the window of my house, I once happened to see some foolish young men. It was late in the evening, sometime after dark. One of these young men turned the corner and was walking by the house of an unfaithful wife. She was dressed fancy like a woman of the street with only one thing in mind. She was one of those women who are loud and restless and never stay at home, who walk street after street, waiting to trap a man. She grabbed him and kissed him, and with no sense of shame she said: "I had to offer a sacrifice, and there is enough meat left over for a feast. So I came looking for you, and here you are! The sheets on my bed are bright-colored cloth from Egypt. And I covered it with perfume made of myrrh, aloes, and cinnamon. Let's go there and make love all night. My husband is traveling, and he is far away. He took a lot of money along, and he won't be back home before the middle of the month." And so she tricked him with all of her sweet talk and her flattery. Right away he followed her like an ox on the way to be slaughtered, or like a fool on the way to be punished and killed with arrows. He was no more than a bird rushing into a trap, without knowing it would cost him his life." [Bible for Today's Family. Proverbs 7:6-23]

"Don't let yourself be attracted by the charm and the lovely eyes of someone like that. A woman who sells her love can be bought for as little as the price of a meal. But making love to another man's wife will cost you everything. If you carry burning coals you burn your clothes; if you step on hot coals, you burn your feet. And if you go to bed with another man's wife, you pay the price." [Bible for Today's Family. Proverbs 6:25-29] Thus we see a seductive sexually driven woman trapping an "innocent" young man. And we find it distressing that the Bible would advise that it would be preferable to purchase a prostitute's service for "as little as the price of a meal" instead of yielding to the seductive efforts of a married woman. Were we not to avoid both options?

There is an account in the New Testament John 8:1-11 about a woman caught in the act of adultery. The Pharisees and scribes lead her to Christ and remind him of Moses' law that such women are to be stoned. The writer of the account has no interest whatsoever in the male involved in this sexual misconduct. Perhaps Eve's second curse is the explanation. Perhaps this woman, like the woman in the Proverbs, had seduced an innocent (but foolish) man. The male was viewed as being innocent because he had been trapped by the sexually motivated woman. In the story of David and Bathsheba, the writer has the woman bathing and cleaning herself in the sight of King David. She sees her strategy handsomely rewarded when David succumbs to her guile.

"A woman will take any man for a husband" [New English Bible. Ecclesiasticus 3:21] How can this astonishing statement be explained and understood? Does the writer leave any doubt as to his conviction about the inequality of men and women? Can it be explained in terms of Eve's second curse where any sex is desirable or must it be explained in terms of the writer's very negative evaluation of a woman's level of intelligence? Or is it both? Certainly the same statement with a gender reversal is unthinkable. Many descriptions of the ideal wife are given. She must be (1) beautiful: "A woman's beauty makes a man happy, there is nothing he desires more" [New English Bible. Ecclesiasticus 36:22] (2) hard working: "she toils at her work … sets about her duties with vigor … does not eat the bread of idleness" [New English Bible. Proverbs 31:10-27] (3) submissive to your husband: "you married women, subordinate yourselves as being secondary to and dependent on your husband." [KJV Amplified Holy Bible. 1st Peter 3:1] (4) quiet: A woman must listen "quietly with due submission. I do not permit a woman to be a teacher, nor must a woman domineer over man; she should be quiet. For Adam was created first, and Eve afterwards; and it was not Adam who was deceived; it was the woman" [New English Bible.1 Timothy 2:11-13] (5) reproductive: "But women will be saved by having children." [Bible for Today's Family. 1 Timothy 2:15]

The second curse for Eve is then a difficult one to reconcile with gender equality. It is also difficult to reconcile with male and female sexuality, as we understand them today. Many would now view the sexual motivation of males and females as being equal. Others, including myself, would take the point of view that on final balance it is the male gender that is more cursed with excessive sexual motivation including perversions that associate sexual gratification with violence. Or sexual motivation is misdirected to vulnerable people who cannot prevent the unwanted advances. The pornography industry is directed primarily at the exploitation of this male weakness. Do rapes occur in the Bible? Of course. Did the writers understand the sometimes uncontrollable sexual urges of men? In Daniel and Susanna we read about the very beautiful and devout daughter of Hilkiah. Two elders who had been appointed as judges beheld her and were "obsessed with lust, … wanted to seduce her … were burning with desire" [New English Bible Daniel and Susanna I:7-20] Despite this and many other passages detailing men burning with desire, the curse involving "eagerness, urges, desires and cravings" was solely directed at Eve, the woman.

Now we will proceed to the third curse directed at Eve. This curse, the most damaging curse, institutes the man Adam as the master over Eve, directing that he shall dominate Eve. Gender equality? Absolutely not! The eleventh chapter of the First Corinthians details and expands the full reach of this the third curse. Women must cover their head, but man must not because "he is the image and reflected glory of God. For man was not created from woman, but woman from man. Neither was man created on account of or for the benefit of woman, but woman on account of and for the benefit of man. Therefore, she should be subject to his authority and should have a covering on her head as a symbol of her submission to authority." [KJV Amplified Holy Bible 1 Corinthians 11:7-10]

This submission to man is then expanded. "I want you to know that the head of every man is Christ, the head of a woman is her husband, and the head of Christ is the Father" [New American Bible. Corinthians 11:3]. These words are powerful and nearly self-explanatory. Just as men report to Christ, women report to men. Women, by virtue of their status, dominated by men, have been removed from direct access to Christ. Men can have a relationship with Christ.

Women are one level further removed from Christ. Thus it is with little wonder that we read that women are to stay quiet in church. "And if they want to learn anything, let them ask their husbands at home: for it is a shame for women to speak in the church" [KJV Amplified Holy Bible.1 Corinthians 14:34-35] The collective force of the last two curses against Eve allowed the writer of Ecclesiasticus to state "Woman is the origin of sin … do not allow a bad wife to say what she likes. If she does not accept your control, divorce her and send her away … a silent wife is a gift from the Lord … a willful woman is a shameless bitch" [New English Bible. Ecclesiasticus 25:25-26] And it continues. "For out of the clothes comes the moth, so harm to women comes from women. Better a man's wickedness than a woman's goodness; it is woman who brings shame and disgrace" [New English Bible. Ecclesiasticus 42:13-14].

This attitude to women explains why biblical advice is always given to men, sons or brothers. It also explains the paucity of roles of significance for women in the Bible. It also explains the whimsical appearance of slurs against women in a context not directly involving women. "Then the Lord said to Moses, One last plague I will bring upon Pharaoh and Egypt. After that he will let you go: "he will send you packing as a man dismisses a rejected bride." [New English Bible. Exodus 11:1] A gender reversal is not possible: as a woman dismisses a rejected groom!" Simply unthinkable! Surely we remember "A woman will marry any man"! So why reject a groom? In a similar way Job manages to insert a slur against women. Job has been afflicted with running sores from head to foot so he took a piece of broken pot to scratch himself as he sat among the ashes. Then his wife said to him "Are you still unshaken in your integrity? Curse God and die!" But he answered "You talk as any wicked fool of a woman might talk. If we accept good from God shall we not accept evil?" [New English Bible. Job 2:8-10] Evil from God? A loving God? It is only mildly surprising that Job then continues the story with an intense wish to die, cursing the day he was born, and continues with an anguished, detailed analysis of why he cannot accept evil from God. Job's wife, a totally insignificant entity in the entire book of Job, is mentioned only once more when Job states "I am repulsive to my wife." [KJV Amplified Holy Bible Job 19:17]

Let us see how this attitude to women permeates the biblical accounts of the three great ancestors of the Israelites, Abraham, Isaac and Jacob. The very well known account becomes of interest here when, forced by a famine, Abram went to Egypt. He tells his wife "I know very well that you are a beautiful woman and that when the Egyptians see you, they will say "She is his wife," then they will kill me but let you live. Tell them that you are my sister so that all may go well with me and my life may be spared." [New English Bible. Genesis 12: 11-13] Things did indeed go well for Abram with his very beautiful wife taken as wife by the Pharaoh and Abram rewarded with sheep, cattle, asses and slaves. Then, struck by grave disease on account of Abram's wife, the Pharaoh sent Sarai back to Abram who then departed Egypt with all his wealth. Was Sarai "used" in Abram's scheme to enrich himself in Egypt? What is astonishing and shocking is that what Abram did was not considered in any way wrong or evil. In the prayer of Manasseh we read "So thou Lord God of the righteous, didst not appoint repentance for Abraham, Isaac and Jacob, who were righteous and did not sin against thee." [New English Bible. Manasseh 1:8]

In accord with God's previous promise to make Abram into a great nation with more descendants than stars, God now made a covenant promising Abram's descendants the land from the River of Egypt to the Euphrates River. Shortly after, God reiterates his promise for land, now indicating a special bond. I will be your God and your descendants God.

For your part, you must keep my covenant and your descendants after you, generation by generation. "This is how you shall keep my covenant between myself and you and your descendants after you: circumcise yourselves, every male among you. … Every uncircumcised male … shall be cut off from the kin of his father. He has broken my covenant." [New English Bible. Genesis 17:9-14] We see that the covenant is between God and exclusively males. What mark shall there be on women to identify them as participants in this covenant?

Next is the subplot in the account of Abraham, as he was renamed at the time of the circumcision, this one dealing with Lot, a relative of Abraham. Sodom and Gomorrah had come to the special attention of the Lord due to all the sin there. To confirm all the negative reports, two angels in man disguise, were assigned to visit Sodom and to determine the actual truth. The two angels were immediately spotted by the only good man in Sodom and they followed his invitation to stay at his house. Lot prepared a meal for them. But before getting to bed they took note of all the young and old men of Sodom gathered around Lot's house. They shouted "Where are the men who came to you tonight? Send them out so that we can have intercourse with them. Lot responded, "No my friends do not be so wicked. Look, I have two daughters, both virgins; let me bring them out to you and you can do what you like with them; but do not touch these men because they have come under the shelter of my roof." [New English Bible. Genesis 19:3-9] Were his daughters not under the shelter of his roof? For his two male visitors the good man Lot provides all he can; sleeping quarters, an opportunity to wash their feet, he made them a dinner complete with drinks and baked unleavened bread. However, he is prepared to send his virgin daughters out to the sleazy, violent, sex crazed rabble to have that rabble "do whatever you like." One can imagine the terror stricken daughters shrinking into a back corner of their home seeking to escape their father's heinous intention. The angels intervene; they strike the rabble blind and they disperse. Next the angels indicate their intention to destroy Sodom and urged Lot to gather his family and leave immediately. They add a specific instruction "Do not look back." Lot's wife, until now, has had no role whatever in this subplot. Now an opportunity for someone to sin, by not following the instruction given earlier, has been put into place. It is in no way surprising that it is Lot's wife that turns back and is, in consequence of her sin, turned into a pillar of salt.

The story continues with Lot going into hiding in a cave with his two daughters. The two daughters then conspire to get their old father drunk in order to get pregnant by him, without him knowing anything about it. It is clear that the good man Lot would never violate the laws against incest. So they make their father drink wine and then each one "went in and lay with her father; and he perceived not when she lay down nor when she arose" [KJV Amplified Holy Bible. Genesis 19:31-35] The daughters had sinned heavily and Lot remained guiltless. Is this sub-sub plot believable? Could the correct story be that Lot drank and then raped his daughters? Did the story get changed to fit the accepted highly negative image of women leaving Lot faultless? This repetitive pattern is certainly clear; evil women and good men.

The account then goes back to Abraham. He settles in Gerar under King Abimelech and yet again, he misinforms the sovereign that Sarah is his sister. She must still be irresistibly beautiful, despite being 90 years old and past child bearing. So the king sent for and took her. In consequence, every woman in Abimelech's household is made barren by God. Abimelech pays 1000 pieces of silver, returns Sarah to Abraham, and with Abraham's intercession, God healed Abimelech and his household. As before, things went well for Abraham.

Isaac was born to the old couple when Abraham was 100 years old. God had stated earlier that it was to be through Isaac that He would fulfill the covenant, an everlasting covenant with his descendants. God blessed Isaac and promised to multiply his descendants and raise a great nation from him. Thus, it must have come as a great shock and surprise to Abraham when God decided to put Abraham to the test saying "Take your son, your only son whom you love, and go to the land of Moriah. There you shall offer him as a sacrifice." [New English Bible. Genesis 22:1-3] Abraham immediately sets about the preparation for fulfilling God's instructions. He is totally unconcerned about the previous promise to raise a great nation from Isaac. How will a dead sacrificed Isaac produce offspring? He is also totally convinced that the instruction from God involves only God, himself and Isaac. Sarah, Isaac's mother, is in no way a participant in this all male business. We know that this subplot ends with an angel of the Lord stopping Abraham's raised arm with knife in hand above his bound son on the alter, on top of the previously split firewood. Again, we must countenance utterly unbelievable cruelty, with trauma inflicted upon Isaac beyond imagining. However, in this context, we are interested in the relationships between women and men and God. And we find that the writer has completely excluded women. Specifically, Sarah, the mother of Isaac is left completely outside of the story. God's test was not directed to a woman but to a man. Killing and sacrificing Isaac had absolutely nothing to do with Sarah. The sacrifice itself had to be a male. The sacrificer also had to be a male. And certainly God was clearly a male. Abraham had passed the test, "Now I know that you are a God-fearing man." [New English Bible. Genesis 22:12] God did not know this before imposing the heinous test? Is God all-knowing? No questions were asked of Sarah before, during or after the test.

Rebecca was to become the wife of Isaac. She was predictably a very beautiful girl. So beautiful that when Isaac was forced by a famine to go to Gerar, still under King Abimelech, he does what his father had done twice before him: Isaac told them that Rebecca was his sister in case they killed him because of her for she was very beautiful.

Rebecca now becomes a very significant player in the next subplot. She prefers Jacob while Isaac prefers Esau. When Isaac was old and his eyesight dim he asked his son Esau to go hunting and prepare a savory dish. Then bring it to me that I may eat it and bless you in the presence of the Lord before I die. Everyone knows what happened next. Rebecca had overheard the previous conversation and now decided to substitute her favorite Jacob in Esau's place in order for Isaac to give the blessing to Rebecca's favorite. Rebecca prepares the savory broth, she gives Jacob Esau's clothes that smelled like Esau, she put goat skins on his hands to feel like Esau's hairy hands. When Jacob fears that this trickery will fail and bring him a curse instead of a blessing she says "Let the curse fall on me my son, but do as I say." [New English Bible. Genesis 27:1-15] The deception works. Isaac recognizes Jacob's voice but the hands feel like Esau's. Repeatedly his son Jacob lies and says "I am Esau your elder son." Then the savory dish was brought which tasted like Esau's and to clinch the deception, when Isaac asked his son to come forward and kiss him, Isaac smelled the smell of Esau's clothes. Rebecca's deceit had worked. Rebecca had played a very significant role. Beautiful yes, but also very evil.

In all of this we will remember Manasseh's statement that all three, Abraham, Isaac and Jacob had no need for repentance, they never sinned. We need to conclude that Jacob's obvious sins (lying to Isaac) were somehow not attributed to him, that they were reflected back to a scheming, deceitful and sinful woman, namely his mother, Rebecca. It seems to have been very useful to have a woman as a partner in the conspiracy who would be fully responsible for all the wrongs done.

The concept of uncleanness was very important to the writers of the Bible. "In this way you shall warn the Israelites against uncleanness in order that they may not bring uncleanness upon the Tabernacle ... and so die" [New English Bible. Leviticus 15:31] "You shall not make yourselves unclean ... for in these ways the heathen, whom I am driving out before you, made themselves unclean. This is how the land became unclean, and I punished it for its iniquity so that it spewed out its inhabitants." [New English Bible. Leviticus 18:24-26] The rules for men to stay clean are relatively light; if he has intercourse with a woman he must bathe his whole body, but will never-the-less stay unclean until evening. The rules for women are more onerous.

"When a woman has a prolonged discharge of blood not at the time of her menstruation, or when her discharge continues beyond the period of menstruation, her impurity shall last all the time of her discharge; she shall be unclean as during the period of her menstruation. Any bed on which she lies during the time of her discharge shall be like that which she used during menstruation, and everything on which she sits shall be unclean as in her menstrual uncleanness. Every person who touches them shall be unclean; he shall wash his clothes, bathe in water and remain unclean til evening. If she is cleansed from her discharge, she shall reckon seven days and after that she shall be ritually clean. On the eighth day she shall obtain two turtle-doves or two young pigeons and bring them to the priest at the entrance to the Tent of Presence. The priest shall deal with one as a sin-offering and with the other as a whole-offering, and make for her before the LORD the expiation required by her unclean discharge." [New English Bible. Leviticus 15: 25-30] The rules, as set out by God, through Moses, for the Israelites, binding for all time, go on to specify some dramatic male female differences.

"The Lord spoke to Moses and said, Speak to the Israelites in these words: When a woman conceives and bears a male child, she shall be unclean for seven days, as in the period of her impurity through menstruation. On the eighth day, the child shall have the flesh of his foreskin circumcised. The woman shall wait for thirty-three days because her blood requires purification; she shall touch nothing that is holy, and shall not enter the sanctuary till her days of purification are completed. If she bears a female child, she shall be unclean for fourteen days as for her menstruation and shall wait for sixty-six days because her blood requires purification. When her days of purification are completed for a son or a daughter, she shall bring a yearling ram for a whole-offering and a young pigeon or a turtledove for a sin-offering to the priest at the entrance to the Tent of Presence. He shall present it before the Lord and make expiation for her and she shall be clean from the issue of her blood. This is the law for the woman who bears a child, whether male or female. If she cannot afford a ram, she shall bring two turtledoves or two young pigeons, one for a whole-offering and the other for a sin-offering. The priest shall make expiation for her and she shall be clean." [New English Bible. Leviticus 12:1-8]

Divorce laws, as given by Moses, are more than discriminatory against women; there are no circumstances that allow a woman to divorce her husband. However, a man is allowed to "write out divorce papers and send his wife away" [New English Bible. Matthew. 19:7] This rule, given earlier by Moses, was rejected by Christ who imposed a new rule. "If your wife has not committed adultery you must not divorce her." [Bible for Today's Family Matthew. 19:9] The reaction of Jesus' disciples to the closing of the door to an easy, uncomplicated divorce is amazing: "Then it is better not to get married." [Bible for Today's Family Matthew 19:10] Was there a picture in the minds of these men of women as the source of all evil; worst of all evils is that of a woman; better a man's wickedness than a woman's goodness?

Moses not only established the rule of easy divorces, he utilizes this rule himself. With absolute ease, Moses "dismissed his wife Zipporah" [New English Bible. Exodus 18:2] leaving her and their two sons in her father Jethro's care. Jethro then goes on to rejoice at all the good the Lord had done for the Israelites. The most callous account of men divorcing or dismissing their wives occurs in Ezra. The reason for this mass dismissal of all these "women and their brood" is God's relentless anger because His "holy race has been contaminated" [New Jerusalem Bible. Ezra 9:2] Ezra beseeches his people to uphold God's commandments and terminate totally any intermarriage with Canaanites, Egyptians, Hittites, etc. The final solution is reported as follows:

"While Ezra was praying and making confession, prostrate in tears before the house of God, a very great crowd of Israelites assembled round him, men, women, and children, and they all wept bitterly. Then Shecaniah son of Jehiel, one of the family of Elam, spoke up and said to Ezra, We have committed an offence against our God in marrying foreign wives, daughters of the foreign population. But in spite of this, there is still hope for Israel. Now, therefore, let us pledge ourselves to our God to dismiss all these women and their brood, according to your advice, my lord, and the advice of those who go in fear of the command of our God; and let us act as the law prescribes. Up now, the task is yours, and we will support you. Take courage and act."

Ezra stood up and made the chiefs of the priests, the Levites, and all the Israelites swear to do as had been said and they took the oath. Then Ezra left his place in front of the house of God and went to the room of

Jehohana, grandson of Eliashib, and lodged here; he neither ate bread nor drank water, for he was mourning for the offence committed by the exiles who had returned. Next, there was issued throughout Judah and Jerusalem a proclamation that all the exiles should assemble in Jerusalem, and that if anyone did not arrive within three days, it should be within the discretion of the chief officers and the elders to confiscate all his property and to exclude him from the community of the exiles. So all the men of Judah and Benjamin assembled in Jerusalem within the three days; and on the twentieth day of the ninth month the people all sat in the forecourt of the house of God, trembling with apprehension and shivering in the heavy rain. Ezra the priest stood up and said, "You have committed an offence in marrying foreign wives and have added to Israel's guilt. Make your confession now to the Lord the God of your fathers and do his will, and separate yourselves from the foreign population and from your foreign wives." Then all the assembled people shouted in reply, "Yes; we must do what you say. But there is a great crowd of us here in the open. Besides, this business will not be finished in one day or even two, because we have committed so grave an offence in this matter. Let our leading men act for the whole assembly, and let all in our cities who have married foreign women present themselves at appointed times, each man with the elders and judges of his own city, until God's anger against us on this account is averted." Only Jonathon, son of Asahel, and Jahzeiah, son of Tikvah, supported by Meshullam and Shabbethaie the Levite, opposed this.

So the exiles acted as agreed, and Ezra the priest selected certain men head of households representing their families, all of them designated by name. They began their formal inquiry into the matter on the first day of their inquiry into all the marriages with foreign women."[New English Bible. Ezra 10:1-17]

Ezra concludes his heart wrenching account listing all the men who were guilty of marrying foreign women with disgusting practices. All listed men "had married foreign women and they dismissed them together with their children." [New English Bible. Ezra 10:44]

Thus God, through Ezra, commands the listed men to dismiss "these women and their brood." Why is there no mention of this in connection to Israelite women who married foreign men? In the context of our Bible it would be utterly impossible to find it written "the listed women were to dismiss their husbands and their brood." The status of women simply did not match the status of men; women were not allowed to dismiss men.

Next we will journey through the book of Esther. We will be overjoyed and then saddened by the appearance of the first feminist of the Bible, a woman who stood her ground, in front of powerful men, and said loudly and clearly "No!" She then was the first woman to publicly repudiate the third curse issued to Eve; to be dominated by a man, Ahasuerus, the Persian King, her husband. I highly recommend that you read the full nine page account of Esther; never-the-less I will summarize it for you here.

It begins with King Ahasuerus hosting a major festivity with white curtains, violet hangings fastened to silver rings, mosaic pavement of alabaster, mother of pearl and turquoise. Wine was served in golden cups. It was served generously. After seven days of this luxurious feasting the king, merry with wine, asked his seven eunuchs to bring Queen Vashti before him in order to display her beauty to the people and the officers. For she was indeed a beautiful woman. One can only speculate what reasons she may have had: would she be required to do the dance of the seven veils? Did she object to putting herself on display as a sex object? Would there be shameless leering? Would it all end in a drunken orgy with violence added for good measure? Or had she entertained the heretical desire to reverse roles: she would command (!) her husband to make an immediate appearance before her and her "harem sisters" to perform the dance of the seven simple soldiers to the leering, jeering peels of derisive laughter of the assembled ladies? But the answer she gave is beyond speculation. She refused her husband's command. The resulting panic among the men is worth reading in its original form.

"Then the king conferred with his wise men versed in misdemeanors; for it was his royal custom to consult all who were versed in law and religion, those closest to him being Carshena, Shethar, Admatha, Tarshish, Meres, Marsena, and Memucan, the seven princes of Persia and Media who had access to the king and held first place in the kingdom. He asked them, "What does the law require to be done with Queen Vashti for disobeying the command of King Ahasuerus brought to her by the eunuchs?" Then Memucan made answer before the king and the princes: "Queen Vashti has done wrong, and not to the king alone, but also to all the officers and to all the peoples in all the provinces of King Ahasuerus. Every woman will come to know what the queen has done; and this will make them treat their husbands with contempt; they will say, "King Ahasuerus ordered Queen Vashti to be brought before him and she did not come." The great ladies of Persia and Media, who have heard of the queen's conduct will tell all the king's officers about this day, and there will be endless disrespect and insolence! If it please your majesty, let a royal decree go out from you and let it be inscribed in the laws of Persians and Medes, never to be revoked, that Vashti shall not again appear before King Ahasuerus; and let the king give her place as queen to another woman who is more worthy of it than she. Thus when the royal edict is heard through the length and breadth of the kingdom, all women will give honour to their husbands, high and low alike." Memucan's advice pleased the king and the princes, and the king did as he had proposed. Letters were sent to all the royal provinces, to every province in its own script and to every people in their own language, in order that each man might be master in his own house and control all his own womenfolk." [New English Bible. Esther 1:13-22]

The standard expectation of every man, Israelite or otherwise, was that the man would dominate over the woman. Therefore, Queen Vashti had to be replaced with a more worthy woman, an obedient woman. Our courageous first feminist of the Bible never again appeared before the king; she disappeared in some hidden backroom of the harem quarters, and was never heard from again.

Her disappearance, however, created an opening for a new queen.

Mordecai, an Israelite living in Susa, heard that beautiful young virgins were to be brought to the king after six months of preening with oil, myrrh, perfumes and cosmetics. Then the king would personally evaluate the girl over the course of an entire night, and then finally, choose from among the girls a replacement for his dismissed queen. Mordecai became quite interested because he sensed an opportunity to slip an undercover agent into the highest level of power and information. He had a cousin, Esther, that he had adopted after her parents had died. She was both beautiful and obedient. And Mordecai was both callous and aggressively ambitious. He would do everything he could to get Esther into the king's harem, preferable into the elevated position of Queen of the King of Persia. Part of this strategy was for Esther never to reveal her Israelite background. The plan succeeded. Mordecai continued to tell Esther exactly what to do, and she, now in the extremely vulnerable and influential role of member of the king's harem, continued in total obedience to Mordecai. In all of this, Mordecai remained utterly unconcerned that harem life for Esther might be unpleasant, sinful, cruel, humiliating or worse.

The king then appointed a new chief officer, Haman, and everyone in the king's court had to bow down to him. But Mordecai was both unbelievably arrogant and insolent and foolish besides. He did two things; he informed them he was a Jew and refused to bow down to Haman. Predictably, Haman was infuriated and resolved to kill Mordecai, and then expanded his wrath to include all of Mordecai's fellow Israelites. Haman received agreement from the king and started making plans for the extermination of the Israelites. Mordecai, now desperate, asked Esther to use her influence over the king to avert the disaster awaiting the Israelites. She then approached the king without being summoned by him, risking her life in doing so. But the king was pleased to see her and agreed to her invitation for himself and Haman to attend a banquet prepared by her. Haman left this meeting only to pass Mordecai, who with his peoples and Esther's life in the balance, again refused to bow down. If Mordecai could conspire to put Esther into the king's harem why could he not bow down to Haman? Haman was so angry that he had a 75 foot high gallows immediately built to be used to terminate Mordecai. The story continues through several convolutions ending up with Mordecai replacing Haman as chief officer and Haman being hanged on the gallows built by Mordecai. The king then signed letters "granting permission to the Jews in every city to … destroy, slay, and exterminate … any people which might attack them, killing women and children too, and to plunder their possessions." [New English Bible. Esther 8:11] On the 13th day of Adar the Israelites took vengeance on their enemies killing seventy five thousand. On the 14th day of Adar the Israelites celebrated and feasted, and still do so, calling this festival the Days of Purim. A beautiful and obedient woman working on behalf of an arrogant, insolent and foolish man accomplished great things for the Israelites.

It is noteworthy that this particular part of Holy Scriptures, the Book of Esther, was not held in high regard by Martin Luther. He said of it "Es ist wertlos", meaning "It is worthless." He was not concerned about gender discrimination issues at all. He was very concerned about the fact that in the entire book of Esther, God is not mentioned once. The active, devious and callous brain pulling all the strings for all the puppets is Mordecai's brain. It is even more noteworthy that the entire book of Esther is retold in the Apocrypha, this time inserting God as the prime conspirator. In that edition, to avoid the idea that Mordecai, the Israelite hero, is arrogant and insolent, Mordecai is here reported as praying "Thou knowest Lord that it was not from insolence, arrogance or vainglory that I refused to bow before proud Haman … I did it because I bow only before Thee" [New English Bible Esther 45 (Apoc) 13:12-23] So Mordecai was justified in not bowing down before Haman. Mordecai did not even consider attempting to justify manipulating the obedient Esther into the harem. It didn't even occur in his mind. Perhaps, as in the previous case of Ezra and the many dismissed women, "contamination of the holy race" occurs only when a Jewish male marries a foreign female; certainly not when a Jewish woman is manipulated into a Persian harem. As we shall see in the next book, Judith, a very devout Israelite woman, had no problem at all prostrating herself and bowing down before the detested leader of the Assyrian forces, Holophernes.

The book of Judith is found in the Apocrypha. The Assyrians, under the leadership of Holophernes, together with other foreign gentile forces, had laid siege to the Israelite city of Bethulia; they had cut off the water supply to the city, and the citizens were in open rebellion against Ozias, the Israelite leader for not having immediately and peacefully surrendered to Holophernes. Of course once the Israelites had indicated their intention to fight and resist, Holophernes made clear his intention to "wipe them off the face of the earth." With food and water fast running out after 34 days of being blockaded, surrounded by enemy forces, "their courage failed." Ozias pleaded with the citizens of Bethulia for five more days of resistance.

Into the midst of this doom and dejection, Judith, a very wealthy and devout Israelite widow, injects herself. She invites the leadership of Bethulia to her estate and chastises them for lack of faith. Further she tells them that she has a secret plan to "take vengeance on our enemies." She then prays asking God's support in taking vengeance on those "foreigners who had stripped off a virgins veil to defile her, uncovered her thighs to shame her and polluted her womb to dishonour her." [New English Bible Judith, Apocrypha, 9:2] Isn't this what happened at Mordecai's bidding to the beautiful virgin Esther? Isn't this what Lot had in mind for his two daughters?

Judith proceeds into her plan. "She removed the sack cloth she was wearing, took off her widow's weeds, then she washed and anointed herself with rich perfume. She did her hair, put on a head band and dressed in her gayest clothes … . She put on sandals and anklets, bracelets and rings, her earrings and all her ornaments and made herself very attractive so as to catch the eye of any man." [New English Bible. Judith, Apocrypha 10:3-5] We are getting an inkling as to what her secret plan is all about. With her maid in tow, she has a gate to Bethulia opened and she walks, head held high, toward the Assyrian forces. She reports to them that she has deserted from the Israelites, that she will provide information to Holophernes how best to defeat the Israelites, stating "For I, your servant, am a religious woman, day and night I worship God" [New English Bible. Judith, Apocrypha 11:17] Never have the Assyrians seen a more ravishing woman. "Her wonderful beauty made them think that the Israelites must be a wonderful people … Who can despise a nation which has such women as this?" [New English Bible. Judith, Apocrypha 10:19] She is brought before Holophernes and she prostrated herself and did obeisance to him. She reveals her traitorous plan to defeat the Israelites impressing Holophernes and all his attendants with her wisdom and her unmatched beauty of face and shrewdness of speech.

A banquet is immediately held. Judith again dressed herself up and put on all her feminine finery. She ate and drank with Holophernes. And her sexual magnetism had its desired effect. "He shook with passion and was filled with ardent desire." Still he remained a gentleman. Holophernes, as in the film Indecent Proposal, the billionaire who had purchased the lovely Demi Moore for one night, stated "nothing will happen without your complete agreement." In retrospect, it speaks volumes for the Assyrian general who self imposes a sexual morality that is exemplary even for the twentieth century. A beautiful woman beguiles him with every means at her disposal and he, a military leader with alcohol in his system, in a time and culture of considerable latitude, restrains himself. Sex only if fully consensual! She accompanies him to his private sleeping quarters. Holophernes continues drinking and with Judith still not yielding, he falls into a deep drunken sleep. Her plan springs into action. After a short prayer asking for strength from the Lord God of Israel, she grabs Holophernes's sword and decapitates him. Two well aimed hacks to his neck do the job. With his head in her food bag, she and her maid make their way back to Bethulia. Judith and all the Israelites rejoice. "The Lord has struck him down by the hand of a woman … though my face lured him to destruction, he committed no sin with me and my honour is unblemished." [New English Bible. Judith, Apocrypha 13:16] Judith's honour required of her only that she not have "polluting" sex. Deceit and the murder of a gentile enemy of the Israelites? No problem. Is she aware of Esther being manipulated by Mordecai into a Persian harem to experience the "uncovering of her thighs to shame her and polluting her womb to dishonour her"? Ozias also is beside himself in a rapturous high. "My daughter, the blessing of God Most High is upon you, you more than all other women on earth, praise be to God … who guided you when you struck off the head of the enemy commander" [New English Bible. Judith, Apocrypha, 13:18] Viewed from the Israeli side, Judith was God fearing, virtuous, blessed, intelligent, articulate, cold blooded and extremely beautiful. However, viewed from the foreign Gentile side we can agree that she was cold blooded, unscrupulous, deceitful, an irresistible temptress flaunting her sexual magnetism, a polished liar and an extremely beautiful woman. Viewed from this side, one might agree with the Book of Sirach "No venom greater than that of a woman" [New English Bible. Sirach, Apocrypha, 25:14] It is noteworthy here that Christ's dictate to love your enemy has no meaning and no relevance, and would be considered laughable or a sign of insanity. Unspeakable crimes committed by Israelites against enemies of Israel were virtuous acts, and when these crimes resulted in heavy fatalities on the enemy's side, there was absolute certainty that God has blessed those crimes. We are left with an image of the woman, Judith, as the conjunction of extreme beauty and extreme evil, the conjunction of consummate visual appeal and consummate concealed wickedness.

We now proceed to the gospels. How did Christ's brief sojourn on the earth affect the status of women? I have no doubt that it was his intention to raise their status, to reduce the injustices against women and to minimize the incidence of divorce. We know that, although he emphatically supports Moses Law [Matthew 5] he rejects Moses Law with respect to divorce and swearing of oaths. In Matthew 5:17-20 he advocates absolute obedience to every letter of the Mosaic Law and goes on to expand that law. He quotes Exodus and Deuteronomy "Thou shalt not commit adultery" and now expands it to "Whosoever looketh on a woman to lust after her hath committed adultery … [Matthew 5:27-28] Then he goes on in the next verse to detail what should be done to the eye that beheld that woman and produced lusty thoughts: pluck it out and throw it away! Fortunately no one takes this directive seriously or we would have many one eyed evangelists! However the weakness of this directive from Christ has had the effect of similarly weakening his following directives, and deletions from the Mosaic Law. "Whosoever dismisses his wife must give her a certificate of divorce" was changed into "divorce is not allowed at all except for the cause of fornication." His disciples were aghast. If we cannot easily dismiss a wife, then it is better not to get married at all! What a tremendous change from the Mosaic Law: "if you see a comely woman among the captives … you may marry her. But if you no longer find her pleasing, let her go … [New English Bible, Deuteronomy 21:10-14] Christ goes on to say " …stay single for the sake of heaven. Anyone who can accept this teaching should do so" [Matthew 19:12] While Christ's purpose here appears to be an encouragement for men to deal responsibly with their wives, it contains a profound and dark foreboding of what we will later find in Revelations. "Stay single for the sake of heaven" will take on very ugly significance.

Christ's choices for membership in his inner sanctum of discipleship excluded women. While he counted women among his friends, there is no indication of any intimacy with any of them. He certainly did not get married. Modern books like The DaVinci Code speculate that Christ was married and that a child was born to him and Mary Magdalene.

What is most troubling in the gospels is the treatment Christ gives one particular woman, his mother. While he embraces the Deuteronomic requirement to respect mother and father, he showed disrespect in the extreme on at least three occasions. Jesus was told "your mother and brothers are standing outside and want to talk with you." Jesus answered "Who is my mother and who are my brothers?" Then he pointed to his disciples and said "They are my mother and brothers." [Matthew 12:47-49] There are cults that see a breaking of family ties as the first order of business in the brainwashing process of their fresh recruits. Here we see Christ rejecting his mother; he indicated a substitution for her, and refused her request to see him. It really is quite disturbing and one's heart goes out to the wronged mother. Respect? I think not. This remarkable and depressing story is given three times, once in each of the first three gospels.

The second occasion of disrespect takes place in connection with his first sign at the Cana wedding. Mary informs him that they have run out of wine. His response to his mother was:

"Woman, how does this concern of yours involve me?"

[New American Bible. John 2:4]

OR

"Woman, what do you want from me? My hour has not yet come." [New Jerusalem Bible. John 2:4]

OR

"Woman what have I to do with thee? Mine hour is not yet come."

[KJV: Amplified Holy Bible. John 2:4]

OR

"You must not tell me what to do, my time has not yet come."

[Good News Bible, John 2:4]

OR

"Your concern, mother, is not mine. My hour has not yet come."

[New English Bible, John 2:4]

OR

"I can't help you now, it isn't yet my time for miracles."

[The Book. John 2:4]

I can well imagine the pain in the minds of the translators of the Bible. How can a son refer to his mother as woman? Does he object to the knowledge that she once sustained his life by an umbilical chord, that she gave him life, that she suckled him at her breasts? Could it be that he is embarrassed to be the offspring of a woman who was pregnant prior to the time of her marriage? Or could it be that he has already rejected her as his mother and has substituted his disciples for his mother? None of these options are nice. Some translators simply could not "stomach" his use of the word woman and changed it to mother. Others, similarly troubled, have managed to uncover an obscure Greek source [Greek Lexicon, Abbott-Smith] making the Greek term woman into a respectful title. I can only ask you if you would ever, being face-to-face with your mother call her woman? The problem was sufficiently darkly perplexing to the translators of The Book that they deemed it the least offensive if they deleted the word woman totally from Jesus' response.

The insolent tone and substance of Jesus' statement continued. He makes it clear that her concerns are not his concerns. Does he feel that this woman's concerns are trivial, childish, foolish or even sinful? In this particular case we might well agree with such an assessment: miraculously creating 150 gallons of quality wine for people who have already "drunk freely" seems an incredibly poor choice for a first miracle with a world suffering in multiple dimensions all around him. It remains a condescending and offensive attitude to his mother.

All the translations make it clear that Jesus does not intend to involve himself in Mary's concerns. It is stated clearly in all translations that "my time has not yet come." Any yet only two lines further, Jesus says "Fill the six jars (25 gallons each) with water and the miracle is consummated. Of course Jesus knew what he was going to do. He did not have to pretend to have an instantaneous and profound change of mind and heart: "my time has not yet come" changes to "my time is here and your concerns are also my concerns".

The third occasion of Jesus' disrespect for his mother occurs near the end of the gospel according to John. Jesus is dying, tortured horribly on the cross and he sees his favorite disciple next to his mother. He says: "Woman, this is your son," and to the disciple he says "This is your mother." [The New Jerusalem Bible. John 19:26-27] OR "Mother here is your son. … There is your mother" [New English Bible. John 19:26-27] OR "He is your son … she is your mother." [The Book. John 19:26-27]

Here again the troubled translators followed similar paths as before. My personal point of view here is that the original manuscripts are in error. Jesus is in the torturous throws of death and it would utterly deny his humanity, to, at that moment refer to his mother as woman. And to indicate to his disciple, in his mother's hearing, that she is now to be his mother, when he has previously rejected her as his mother is deeply troubling and offensive again.

The gospel of John includes the story of Jesus and the adulterous woman. Pharisees and scribes bring the defendant to Jesus, saying they caught her in the act of adultery. They remind him of the Mosaic Law penalty for that crime, death by stoning. Expecting to trap Jesus they asked him "What do you have to say about this case?" What answer were the Pharisees expecting that would have "sprung the trap?" It appears that the answer he gave should have sprung that trap. Jesus said "Let him who is without sin be the first to cast a stone." Then, if the Mosaic Law was to be obeyed, Jesus would have had to throw the first stone. Mercifully, he did not, and the original accusers, finding themselves with sin, could not throw the first stone and one by one they left. The Mosaic Law was no longer in effect because of Christ's brand new, unprecedented requirement for the enforcers: Christ required the thrower of the first stone to be free from sin. Where exactly could enforcers be found that would satisfy the requirement to be free from sin? With no one free from sin no law could be enforced. With no enforcement possible, the laws have effectively been scrapped. If the Pharisees wanted a statement from Christ making him vulnerable they got it. But instead of utilizing the sprung trap, they simply depart.

It is good to see Christ deal mercifully with the adulterous woman. But we are extremely troubled by the fact that Christ raises no question whatever about the second party to the adultery. What about the male also caught in the act? Did he benefit from the well known double standard? Did he get seduced? Was he an important person, who was thus above the law? We know from the Old Testament [Genesis 38] that when widowed Tamar felt she had been wronged by her father-in-law, Judah, she disguised herself; she pretended to be a prostitute and Judah purchased her services, leaving his seal, cord and staff with her to guarantee payment. She conceived. Three months later it came to Judah's attention that his widowed daughter-in-law, Tamar, had become pregnant, that she had committed adultery. Judah, the all powerful patriarch, immediately pronounced the sentence: death by burning. Then she revealed the seal, cord and staff of the man she had committed adultery with; everyone recognized the seal, cord and staff of Judah. Now that Judah was involved, the law against adultery vanished like a mist over the Sahara Desert when the sun rises. Though both were clearly guilty of adultery, all penalties are waived, and Judah magnanimously promises to cease having intercourse with Tamar.

It is noteworthy in the story of John, Chapter 8 that when all the sinners have left, and Christ is alone with the accused female, he addresses her as follows "Woman, where are your accusers?" This is the same form of address that he used for his own mother at the wedding at Cana and in his final moments on the cross.

We have already seen the gender discrimination related passages of the Acts and letters in the New Testament. We remember women serve men, men serve Christ, and Christ serves God. We remember the disbarment of women from teaching and from leadership roles in the church. Several times we were reminded that Adam was created first, and Eve sinned first.

It is however, in the Revelations part of the New Testament that we are shocked by the most damaging statement against women in the entire Bible. It is introduced when Peter asks in Matthew 19:27 "We have left everything to be your followers. What will we get?" And Christ answers that in the future you, that is his twelve disciples, will "sit on twelve thrones to judge the twelve tribes of Israel." [Matthew 19:29] The Cree, Cheyenne, Italians, Japanese … seem to have been excluded. Only the Israelites are eligible for judging? It is again introduced when we read in Matthew 19:12 "stay single for the sake of heaven." But these introductions do precious little to prepare us for what we will have to read in Revelations. It begins with "Don't harm the earth or the sea or any tree! Wait until I have marked the foreheads of the servants of our God." Identifying marks are to be inscribed on the foreheads of God's Servants. [Revelations 7:3] This is foreshadowed in Ezekiel 9:4-7: "Walk through the streets of Jerusalem and put a mark on the foreheads of the <u>men</u> who groan and lament because of all the sins they see around them. The Lord God then gave the command "spare not nor pity them, kill them all, old and young, girls, women and little children, but don't touch anyone with the mark." [Ezekiel 9:5-6] Again, the Biblical tendency to barbaric extremes of violence and bloodletting can be seen. But in addition we see again in Ezekiel the blatant preference given to males versus females. How many women got the mark on their foreheads?

We continue in Revelations. How many people are to get the mark? The number was counted with extreme precision, exactly 144,000! It is only mildly surprising then, when this number is subdivided into exactly 12,000 from each of the twelve tribes of Israel. These numbers of course fall squarely into the realm of numerology, the occult notion that certain numbers are more propitious or acceptable to God than other numbers. But the question burning now in our minds is: how many women, if any, will be among the 144,000 blessed with the mark? This answer is given as follows: "The 144,000 people stood before the throne, the four living creatures and the elders; they were singing a new song which <u>only</u> they could learn. Of all mankind, they are the <u>only</u> ones who have been redeemed. They are the <u>men</u> who have kept themselves pure by not having sexual relations with women; they are virgins. … they are faultless." [<u>Good News</u>

Bible. Revelations 14:3-5] OR "These are they who have not defiled themselves with women, they are virgins." [KJV Amplified Holy Bible. Revelations 14:4-5] OR … the 144,000 who had been ransomed from the world. These are men who have never been defiled by immorality with women. They are pure … they are indeed without flaw." [New American Bible. Revelations 14:3-5] OR … the 144,000 who alone from the whole world had been ransomed. These are men who did not defile themselves with women, for they have kept themselves chaste … ." [New English Bible. Revelations 14:3-5]

We have started with the three curses against Eve and now, at the very end of the Bible, we find only men among the 144,000 who alone from the whole world have the required identifying mark. Never before was there such a clear exclusion of women. Is this what "women serve men and men serve Christ" is really all about? Are men in a duly sanctified marriage relationship with a woman automatically to be excluded? The writers of The Book found themselves again in dramatic disagreement with the original manuscript. They changed it to read "the 144,000 are spiritually undefiled, as pure as virgins."

After reading that these 144,000 are the only ones who have been ransomed from the whole earth, it doesn't help much to read the contradictory statements "Then I saw a vast throng … from every nation … robed in white." [New English Bible. Revelations 7:9-14] Is the number 144,000 now irrelevant? Is the mark on the forehead now nice to have, but a white robe is just as good? Does the statement "the only ones who have been ransomed from the whole earth" mean anything? Can we throw out the number 144,000 and keep a vast throng? Does the contradiction invalidate both?

As before with Abraham and all the patriarchs, and Ezekiel and Job, etc., God's role in his relationship with humanity was an intense relationship with a handful of favored males, and a minimal relationship with non favored males and all females. In the example of Job, God views him to be significant; Job's male advisors are of lesser significance, Job's sons and daughters and wife of no significance whatever. God's vision for humanity as revealed in the inspired book, the Bible, does not include gender equality.

Before we can leave the issue of gender discrimination we must revisit the story of Lot and his two virgin daughters. This depressing story is retold in the Bible in a different setting with new characters. A Levite had "taken himself" a concubine and had, as we shall have reason to understand later, maltreated her. She left him and went back to her father's house. After four months the Levite set out after her. The Levite was well received and well entertained. The girl's father and the Levite ate and drank amicably together for five days. Finally, the Levite, with his concubine, left to go back to the Levite's home. On route they arrive at the Benjaminite town Gibeah. An old man invited them to spend the night at his house. While the Levite and the old man were enjoying themselves, eating and drinking, the scoundrels of Gibeah gathered outside the house and started battering on the door. "Bring out the strange man who has gone into your house for us to have intercourse with him. The old man, the owner of the house, went outside and said "No my friends, do nothing so wicked. This man is my guest; do not commit this outrage. Here is my daughter, a virgin, let me bring her out to you. Rape her, and do to her what you please. But you shall not commit such an outrage against this man." [New English Bible. Judges 19:21-25] These words are both depressing and enraging. Sodomy with the man is clearly an outrage but raping and sodomizing the virgin daughter is an acceptable alternative?

The story continues. The scoundrels outside kept up their clamour and with a slight change of plans by the old man and the Levite, the virgin daughter is kept inside, and the Levite "thrusts" his concubine outside, into the hands of the scoundrels. They "raped and assaulted" her all night and finally when dawn broke they let her go. She crawled back to the old man's house and collapsed at the door. Nobody was waiting anxiously for her return. All remained quiet in the house. Finally her master, the Levite, rose from his sleep, opened the door, and there was his concubine "lying at the door with her hands on the threshold." He said to her "Get up and let us be off." The criminal callousness of this man, in his treatment of this pitiable woman, simply knows no bounds. If ever there was reason to stone someone, the Levite deserves it. The women, both the virgin daughter of the old man and the concubine wife of the Levite, were given absolutely no control over their own lives; they were under the full and unfettered control of the men in their lives. And these men dealt with these women as a sub-species not as human beings. Their well-being, health, pain, their suffering were of no relevance in the minds of these men. And these men are given a moral all clear signal throughout this entire Bible story: they are, in the context of these monstrous, heinous and barbaric actions, faultless.

The story continues. When the girl doesn't answer, we are left with the open ended question is she alive or dead? The Levite does not seem to care. He loads her onto one of his donkeys and takes her to his home. He then cuts her up into twelve pieces sending her dismembered body to all parts of Israel to encourage punitive action against the Benjaminites. They refuse to turn over the scoundrels who raped the girl. The Israelites then go to war against all Benjaminites killing all men, all women, and all children, leaving only 600 men who escape into the hills. What role exactly did the women and children play in the crime against the concubine? Now that only 600 men are left, and they have no wives, the Israelites realize that the number of Israelite tribes is about to be reduced from the sacred number 12 to the unacceptable number 11. The Israelites violate a "great oath" that they have previously made and rush off to Jabesh-Gilead where they kill all men and non virgin women, and all children retaining 400 virgins for the Benjaminites. The remaining 200 bachelor Benjaminites are then encouraged to hide in the vineyard of Shiloh, and when the girls come out to dance simply grab or seize one to be your wife. Problem solved. Any inconvenience or pain for women: irrelevant! And the magic number of 12 Israelite tribes: still in effect! It is not a pretty scene. Gender discrimination? Ask any mother, sister, daughter or wife!

Epilogue to Gender Discrimination

The curses outlined in Genesis sought to explain what people saw all around them: the hated snakes scurrying on the ground "eating dust," the ever present weeds and thistles the keeper of the fields encountered. The three curses against Eve served the same purpose. We remind ourselves of the three curses:

1) painful childlbirth
2) intense sexual motivation
3) domination by males in general and by the husband in particular.

These curses were then descriptors of the female condition.

The males who analyzed the status of the females understood all three descriptors of females as extremely damaging to women. Thus, the explanation for the origin of the female condition took the form of curses imposed by God. Blessings produce happy, healthy, supportive and painfree results. Curses produce the opposite. The Garden of Eden story provided an acceptable explanation for the people of that time. God was angered, in particular at Eve, for violating his dictate "Do not eat from the Tree of Knowledge of Good and Evil." God then vented his fury at Eve in the three curses.

The first curse, as a descriptor of the female condition finds instant resonance with us. All those males who have experienced the pangs of childbirth at the side of their wife will have at least some vicarious notion of the pain that is involved. Why so much pain? The Genesis story traces it back to the wrath of God at Eve: "In pain shall you bear your children."

The third curse that a woman shall be dominated by her husband finds a bit less immediate resonance with us. Moslems would argue, with at least some women in sincere agreement, that male domination over women is there for everyone's benefit. This point of view would attempt to have women recognize that domination over them by males is actually a blessing. Christian marriage vows for almost two millennia included "Love, cherish and obey … your husband." Here also one senses an attempt to persuade women that obeying your husband would again be a blessing. The authors of Genesis thought otherwise. They cherished their own free and undominated status. And they viewed women's not free and male dominated status as a pitiful state of affairs. Thus they reasoned that their status, dominated by their husband, had to be the consequence of a grievous curse from God. Perhaps they also reasoned that their fervent wish to keep women subservient would be well served, indeed, by making their subservience a consequence of a curse imposed by no mere mortal but by

God himself. It remains noteworthy that the writers of Genesis had an opinion about male domination over females that is identical to the opinion of feminists and many others of male domination over females: it was and is very damaging to women. This viewpoint has lately been expanded: Male domination over females is very damaging to all of us. Accordingly, wedding vows now routinely speak of equal partners. Biblical references with any direct or even indirect suggestion about male dominance - they have been banished.

C. S. Lewis, the foremost Christian philosopher/theologian of the 20th century, has a very clear understanding of the third curse. He takes the point of view that every marriage must confer a veto power upon either the woman or the man. How else shall disputes be resolved? And he goes on to state that it must be the male who will be the head. "Why?" we ask. He thinks that women prefer it that way. "There must be something unnatural about the rule of wives over husbands because the wives themselves are half ashamed of it and despise the husbands whom they rule." [Mere Christianity p100] In his opinion women have an overriding loyalty to their own family while males recognize our membership in the larger family of man. Men are "much more just to the outsiders" [p100] "while women are characterized by intense family patriotism" [p100]. Many Christian women will object to C. S. Lewis's point of view.

Now then, the second curse: eagerness, urges, desires and cravings! This curse finds no resonance with us at all. Should not a strong desire for sex together with a generous capacity to enjoy sex, should this not be considered a blessing?! But if carried to extremes, we might agree that the blessing might be potentially tainted. But women cursed with eagerness … cravings as set apart from men who have not been cursed with eagerness, urges, desires and cravings? We are suddenly assailed by the heretical thought: Did someone play a trick on us by reassigning a curse that God directed against males: could it be that this curse was redirected to apply against women? Every second news item confirms the common knowledge. Yet another male with excessive sexual domination motivations involved in another horrendous crime against a woman. There can be no doubt - we know that it is males that have been cursed with excessive sexual motivation. So why this curse against women? Are we missing something, or is our world in some very significant way, not the same world that the writers of Genesis experienced?

Among the leadership of the Israelites, it was standard practice to have more than one wife. Polygamy was the rule and monogamy was the exception. Thus we expect to see family structuring that includes a harem.

This structure came with certain predictable parameters. It was unthinkable that a woman could ever leave a harem. If she did and got caught, the death penalty would be enforced. The owner of the harem, that is the male with exclusive sexual rights to those women, determined on a "favored status" basis what rank each woman in his harem would be accorded. Abraham's harem included Sarah, Hagar, Keturah and concubines [Genesis 25:5-6], Sarah was ranked number one. Jacob had a harem of four women, Rachel, his favorite, Leah (the dull eyed one) Zilpah and Bilhah. In this harem it is noteworthy that Jacob's favoring of the beautiful, graceful Rachel climaxed in Jacob refusing sex with Leah. She complains to Rachel, "Is it so small a thing to have taken away my husband?" [Genesis 30:15] Leah strikes a deal with Rachel wherein the guid pro quo grants Leah one night with Jacob in return for the fruit of the mandrake to be given to Rachel. The fruit was to come from Leah's son's garden. When Jacob came home that evening, Leah informed him that Rachel had agreed to have him spend the night with her. Of course Leah conceived. We notice that the rank of a woman within the harem confers power upon that woman. The least favored woman can expect a prison existence in the shabbiest quarters with not even an occasional visit from the owner/husband. King Solomon, with a harem of 1000 women, is utterly disgusting. Most of those women could expect to live out their years in a prison existence under constant guard. We know that King Ahasuerus, who included Esther in his harem, let all of his women know that if any of them independently made an appearance before him, they would be subject to immediate execution. It is very clear that for most members of a harem, their life consisted of a sexual slave labor camp.

King David's harem had almost twenty women. Consider the behavior of those women when the rumour was circulated that the master was on his way home from just another military campaign. All the very best of their feminine attire and perfume and paint would be put to work. They certainly know the routine. When the master entered the harem every member of the harem would be in competition to attract, to seduce, to entice the master into her private quarters. What can a woman do to entice a man into her arms and bed when she has competitors all around her? And after the master has succumbed to the superior enticements of one of his women, they know that he has the stamina to "take on" one more, the one that does a superb dance of the seven veils. But after two encounters, the master would actually get angry at any of the remaining women who abjectly continue to try to seduce the fatigued and sated master. It is from this picture of harem life that the writers of Genesis determined that all women had been cursed by God. The picture of all members of the harem trying to outperform each other as sex kittens, as bimbos, as cats in heat, while the cool master samples them visually, easily able to pass up the offered sexual favors, finally bestowing his favors upon the extremely fortunate number one choice - this picture explains the second curse. Harem life, imposed by powerful males, led to a totally distorted image of female sexuality. It is distressing to understand that harem life, complete with its distortion of female sexuality, still accurately describes many societies.

# Chapter 2
# Race:  Israelites Preferred?

**Israelites Preferred?**

Favoritism is not considered a virtuous aspect of any individual, group or country. Evenhandedness, that is the opposite of favoritism, is the basis of all justice. If the king's friends are going to be accorded special status by the king's justice officials, there is no purpose in even attempting to right a wrong. When one child is favored over another by his mother or father, grief is the guaranteed result. Thus, where no mechanism for justice is in place and the dictator, who has chosen his favorites, also ensures preferential treatment for those favorites, the non favorites can only recede into the background to attempt to eke out a living as far away from that dictator as possible. This is, of course, especially true when that dictator is often in a state of anger, wrath, fury, and jealousy, and does not shy away from war crimes, crimes against humanity or genocide and "delights in destroying and exterminating" when his rage has been kindled. [New English Bible. Deuteronomy 28::63]

And yet the fundamental theme of the Old Testament is the favored status of one tribe or group of people, the Israelites. "The Lord your God chose you out of all nations on earth to be his special possession." [New English Bible. Deuteronomy 7:6] This choice by God comes in direct connection with the promise of a land of milk and honey, already occupied by other peoples who happen to be the "unchosen" people, the rejected people. "When the Lord your God brings you into the land which you are entering to occupy and drives out many nations before you - Hittites, Girgashites, Amorites, Canaanites, Perizzites, Hivites, and Jebusites, seven nations more numerous and powerful than you - when the Lord your God delivers them into your power and you defeat them, you must put them to death. You must not make a treaty with them or spare them. You must not intermarry with them, neither giving your daughters to their sons nor taking their daughters for your sons; if you do, they will draw your sons away from the Lord and make them worship other gods. Then the Lord will be angry with you and will quickly destroy you. But this is what you must do to them: pull down their altars, break their sacred pillars, hack down their sacred poles and destroy their idols by fire, for you are a people holy to the Lord your God; the Lord your God chose you out of all nations on earth to be his special possession." [New English Bible. Deuteronomy 7:1-6]

"You shall devour all the nations which the Lord your God is giving over to you. Spare none of them, and do not worship their gods; that is the snare which awaits you. You may say to yourselves, "These nations outnumber us, how can we drive them out?" But you need to have no fear of them; only remember what the Lord your God did to Pharaoh and to the whole of Egypt, the great challenge which you yourselves witnessed, the signs and portents, the strong hand and the outstretched arm by which the Lord your God brought you out. He will deal thus with all the nations of whom you are afraid. He will also spread panic among them until all who are left or have gone into hiding perish before you. Be in no dread of them, for the Lord your God is in your midst, a great and terrible god. He will drive out these nations before you little by little. You will not be able to exterminate them quickly, for fear the wild beasts become too numerous for you. The Lord your God will deliver your nations over to you and will throw them in great panic in the hour of their destruction. He will put their kings into your hands, and you shall wipe out their name from under heaven. When you destroy them, no man will be able to withstand you. Their idols you shall destroy by fire; you must not covet the silver and gold on them and take it for yourselves, or you will be ensnared by it; for these things are abominable to the Lord your God. You must not introduce any abominable idol into your houses and thus bring ourselves under solemn ban along with it. You shall hold it loathsome and abominable, for it is forbidden under the ban" [New English Bible. Deuteronomy 7:17-26] We shall see that the main point of objection against the rejected peoples is that they worship other gods. The Israelite God admittedly is a very "Jealous God." [New English Bible. Exodus 34::15]

We will now go to Exodus, the account of the departure of the Israelites from Egypt. It begins with this statement from God: "The Lord said, 'I have indeed seen the misery of my people in Egypt. I have heard their outcry against their slave-masters. I have taken heed of their sufferings, and have come down to rescue them from the power of Egypt, and to bring them up out of that country into a fine, broad land; it is a land flowing with milk and honey, the home of Caaanites, Hittites, Amorites, Perizzites, Hivites, and Jebusites'." [New English Bible. Exodus 3:7-9] Moses receives his commission to be the leader of the Israelites from God, talking through the medium of a burning bush. Moses protests that he is too "slow and hesitant of speech" to be a leader, and God reluctantly and angrily permits Moses to utilize his brother Aaron to be his mouthpiece. Moses is given instructions by God to approach the Pharaoh of Egypt with the request to "let my people (the Israelites) go." [New English Bible. Exodus 4:21] Here we have a first indication of the full impact of God's favoritism. The Israelites are the favorites, the Egyptians are the rejected ones, and God, instead minimizing pain and suffering, sees an opportunity to display His power and favoritism.

"I have made him and his courtiers obdurate so that I may show these signs among them, and so that you can tell your children and grandchildren the story: how I made sport of the Egyptians, and what signs I showed among them. Thus you will know that I am the Lord." [New English Bible. Exodus 10:1-2] What does "make sport of the Egyptians" mean? What signs would God employ to make sport of the Egyptians? Why does God make the Pharaoh stubborn? We find out immediately what making "sport" means. The water of the Nile was turned into blood, Egypt was swarmed by frogs, all the dust of Egypt was turned into maggots. Then the "sport" turned more violent. The grazing herds of Egypt, horses, asses, camels, sheep and cattle were struck with a pestilence and all died. But in Israel's herds not a single one shall die. Thus the "Lord made a distinction" between Israel and Egypt. Festering boils appeared on the Egyptians. Hail struck the Egyptians and still Pharaoh would not let the Israelites go because, even when he wished to let them go, God interfered in his heart and mind and made him stubborn, to keep the "signs" and the "sport" continuing. Hail and locusts destroyed Egypt. And yet God kept the Pharaoh stubborn to unleash a final plague upon all Egyptians, people and animals alike: At midnight "I will go out among the Egyptians and kill every first born creature in all of Egypt" with the exception of course of his favorites. All first borns then includes the first child in all Egyptian families. The vindictiveness and horror exceed all measure. An Egyptian family living hundreds of miles from Cairo, who have never seen an Israelite, have no opinion on Israelites and clearly have no influence over the Pharaoh, suddenly see the first borns of their flocks die, and then their first born son or daughter also dies. "All of Egypt will send up a great cry of anguish, a cry the like of which has never been heard before, nor ever will be again. But among all Israel not a dog's tongue shall be so much as scratched." [New English Bible. Exodus 11:5-7] Now we know the full extent of the difference between God's favorites, his special possession, his chosen tribe and the Egyptians, the rejected ones. The anguished cry of the Egyptians is the "sport" that God had in mind when he unleashed his final sign. There was no need for the final sign or the previous signs. It was God's choice to "harden Pharaoh's heart" and thus to continue with the signs "so that I may win glory for myself at the expense of Pharaoh" and all Egyptians. [New English Bible. Exodus 14:4] Not a house in Egypt was without its dead.

Now we have an 180° turn in Gods interference. Now he softens the hearts of the Egyptians; he made the Egyptians "well disposed' toward the Israelites. Now, the Israelites asked the anguish stricken Egyptians for "jewelry of gold and silver and, lo behold, the Egyptians let them have what they asked. In this way they plundered the Egyptians." [New English Bible. Exodus 12:36] Whether God hardened Pharaoh's heart or softened the hearts of the Egyptians, it was always done to help his favorites, to bring himself glory at the cost of extreme suffering for the Egyptians. It does pay to be on the chosen side. The story concludes with the parting of the water for the Israelites and the drowning of the Pharaoh and his army.

The next 40 years the Israelites spend in the vicinity of Sinai, with Moses elucidating the laws given to him by God to govern the behavior of the chosen people. A small selection of this myriad of rules includes "Whosoever reviles his father or mother shall be put to death; you shall not suffer (allow) a witch to live; whoever sacrifices to any God but the Lord God Jehovah shall be put to death; you must not mount up to the altar by steps in case your private parts be exposed, etc." While Moses is on the mountain, the Israelites built themselves a golden bull calf and proclaimed it their god and made offerings to it. A primary law of God had been violated. God now takes action against a portion of his own chosen people. Moses said "Who is on the Lord's side? Come here to me; and the Levites all rallied to him. He said to them, 'These are the words of the Lord the God of Israel" "Arm yourselves, each of you, with his sword. Go through the camp from gate to gate and back again. Each of you kill his brother, his friend, his neighbour.'" The Levites obeyed, and about three thousand of the people died that day. Moses then said, 'Today you have consecrated yourselves to the Lord completely, because you have turned each against his own son and his own brother and so have this day brought a blessing upon yourselves.' " [New English Bible. Exodus 32:26-29]
God's expectations of his chosen people are onerous and the penalties for violations are incredibly heavy. A final noteworthy set of laws put in place by Moses reads as follows: "The Lord spoke to Moses and said, speak to Aaron in these words: No man among your descendants for all time who has any physical defect shall come and present the food of his God. No man with a defect shall come, whether a blind man, a lame man, a man stunted or overgrown, a man deformed in foot or hand, or with mis-shapen brows or a film over his eye or a discharge from it, a man who has a scab or eruption or has had a testicle ruptured. No descendant of Aaron the priest who has any defect in his body shall approach to present the food-offerings of the Lord; because he has a defect he shall not approach to present the food of his God. He may eat the bread of God both from the holy-gifts and from the holiest of holy-gifts, but he shall not come up to the veil nor approach the altar, because he has a defect in his body. Thus he shall not

profane my sanctuaries, because I am the Lord who hallows them." [New English Bible. Leviticus 21:16-23]

We will now accompany the Israelites in their quest to take over the promised land. We know that the promised land was already home to many peoples. However, the Caaanites, Hittites, Amorites, Perizzites, Hivites, and Jebusites are not the chosen peoples, they worship other gods. They are the rejected peoples. Here we see a brand new interpretation placed upon the age old competition between man for living space, for a land of milk and honey. History books are full of the stories of how a particular group of people increase their food production, increase their population, devise new weaponry, implement more effective organizational techniques and strategies and then launch wars of conquest. Nations rise and go through the ugly process of defeating, massacring and enslaving and sometimes annihilating another nation. Land changes hands, gods are replaced and cultures are changed. And when that expanded successful nation declines (history books provide an unconditional guarantee that they will decline) they will experience the ravages of wars of conquest this time leaving them on the defeated side. Military might is the essential ingredient.

For the Israelites, their war of conquest is presented as initiated, presided over, orchestrated and determined by their God. Their Lord Jehovah becomes a "warrior" [New English Bible. Exodus 15:3] God becomes the essential ingredient. And the military might of the Israelites is guaranteed by obedience to God's laws. Thus we have the song: "This land is mine - God gave this land to me." A more historically accurate rendering of the song would be: "This land was theirs - We killed them all with ease." These wars of conquest invariably involve human suffering on a grand scale. It is both murder and theft on a grand scale. "The Lord your God will bring you into the land which he swore to your forefathers Abraham, Isaac and Jacob, that he would give you a land of great and fine cities which you did not build, houses full of good things which you did not provide, rock-hewn cisterns which you did not hew, and vineyards and olive-groves which you did not plant. When you eat your fill there, be careful not to forget the Lord who brought you out of Egypt, out of the land of slavery. You shall fear the Lord your God, serve him alone and take oaths in his name. You must not follow other gods, gods of the nations that are around you; if you do the Lord your God who is in your midst will be angry with you, and he will sweep you away off the face of the earth, for the Lord your God is a jealous god." [New English Bible. Deuteronomy 6:10-15]

These are the instructions that God provides for the Israelite conquest:

"When you advance on a city to attack it, make an offer of peace. If the city accepts the offer and opens its gates to you, then all the people in it shall be put to forced labour and shall serve you. If it does not make peace with you but offer to battle, you shall besiege it, and the Lord your God will deliver it into your hands. You shall put all males to the sword, but you may take the women, the dependents and the cattle for yourselves, and plunder everything else in the city. You may enjoy the use of the spoil of your enemies which the Lord your God gives you. That is what you shall do to cities at a great distance, as opposed to those which belong to nations near at hand. In the cities of these nations whose land the Lord your God is giving you as a patrimony, you shall not leave any creature alive. You shall annihilate them - Hittites, Amorites, Caaanites, Perizzites, Hivites, and Jebusites - as the Lord your God commanded you, so that they may not teach you to imitate all the abominable things that they have done for their gods and so cause you to sin against the Lord your God. [New English Bible. Deuteronomy 20:10-18]

Special instructions are given with respect to the women taken as prisoners. God's instruction given in Deuteronomy 7:2-3 not to intermarry with the Caaanites, Hittites, Amorites, Perizzites, Hivites, and Jebusites lest they induce you to the mortal crime of worshipping other gods, is now forgotten. The intense worry about "contaminating the holy race" gives way to God's new instruction, a reversal from the previous: " When you wage war against your enemy and the Lord your God delivers them into your hands, and you take some of them captive, then if you see a comely woman among the captives and take a liking to her, you may marry her. … But if you no longer find her pleasing, let her go … ." [Deuteronomy 21:10-14]

Moses, on his death bed, passes his command to Joshua, the great military strategist. Moses leaves Joshua with this description of the Israelite warrior god: 'See now that, I, I am He, and there is no god beside me: I put to death and I keep alive, I wound and I heal; there is no rescue from my grasp. I lift my hand to heaven and swear: As I live forever; when I have whetted my flashing sword, when I have set my hand to judgment, then I will punish my adversaries and take vengeance on my enemies, I will make my arrows drunk with blood, my sword shall devour flesh, blood of slain and captives, the heads of the enemy princess.' Rejoice with him, you heavens, bow down all you gods, before him; for he will avenge the blood of his sons and take vengeance on his adversaries; he will punish those who hate him and make expiation for his people's land." [New English Bible. Deuteronomy 32:39-43]

Finally, we have Moses giving a summary of God's wondrous works for the Israelites. Jacob is singled out as particularly blessed with wine, meat from his flocks and grain from his fields. But, then the Israelites roused his jealousy [Deuteronomy 32:16 and 21] because they adopted "abominable practices" from their Gentile, pagan neighbors. With his anger provoked, he unleashes hunger, plague, pestilence, wild beasts and poisonous creatures on his chosen people. God then made plans to annihilate his own people: "I had resolved to strike them down and to destroy all memory of them, but I feared … that their enemies would take the credit and say it was not the Lord, it was we who raised the hand that did this." [Deuteronomy 32:26-27] We are expected to believe that God would have annihilated his people, if only he would be given full credit for that annihilation. Sharing credit for that annihilation - that was something God was not prepared to do. Thus, the Israelites were spared.

Joshua then moves his Israelites to his first military objective, the city of Jericho. Joshua, the strategist, does what any military leader would do, he sent two spies with secret orders to reconnoiter the country and the city. With or without God on your side, good intelligence is worth gold. The spies get into Jericho and stay at the house of a prostitute named Rahab. She then lets the spies know the mood of the people of Jericho; it is identical to the mood of Europeans whose small town is in the path of the "barbarians" and their likely fate is the fate of other towns before them: raping, looting, burning and finally killing. "I know that the Lord has given this land to you, the terror of you has descended upon us all, and that because of you the whole country is panic-stricken. For we have heard how the Lord dried up the water of the Red Sea before you when you came out of Egypt, and what you did to Sihon and Og, the two Amorite kings beyond Jordan, whom you put to death. When we heard this our courage failed us." [New English Bible. Joshua 2:9-11] In return for hiding and protecting the spies Rahab and her family are promised that they will be spared. We know the rest: the city fell to the Israelites. Everyone is put to the sword, men, women, and children; their worst fears are realized; only Rahab and her family are spared.

The next objective was the city of Ai. Joshua, the military strategist, dispatched 30,000 fighting men during the night to hide in ambush. He succeeded in luring the defenders of Ai out of their city to give chase, to what they thought was, the defeated Israelites. The people of Ai were defeated, and 12,000 people, the whole population of Ai, men, women and children, were all put to the sword. The king of Ai was hanged "The men of Ai looked back and saw the smoke from the city already going up to the sky; they were powerless to make their escape in any direction, and the Israelites who had feigned flight towards the wilderness turned on their pursuers." [New English Bible. Joshua 8:20] On page 252 and 253 (Joshua 10-11) of the New English Bible, the expression is given in ten different places: "every living thing was put to the sword." The contrast could not be more clear; the chosen ones versus the rejected ones: the victorious versus the defeated; the killers verses the killed. It was the Lord's purpose that they should be annihilated without mercy and utterly destroyed. [Joshua 11:20]

We will notice that nowhere in God's (Israelites) dealings with the non-chosen peoples, is there an attempt made to convert these Gentiles into believers of God Jehovah, into a part of the tribe of the Israelites. Indeed there is a deep implication that membership in the tribe of the Israelites is entirely racial. To be an Israelite you must be a member of one of the twelve tribes, a descendant of one of the twelve sons of Jacob, as they are listed in the Bible from Genesis to Revelations. If you are a Reubenite, or a Simeonite, ... a Levite, a Josephite or a Benjamnite, then you are an Israelite. You are an Israelite if you can claim the three great and holy ancestors, Abraham, Isaac and Jacob. In the words of Jacob, on his deathbed addressing his sons, we read "These then are the twelve tribes of Israel ... and he blessed them each in turn." [New English Bible. Genesis 49:28] Even when the Egyptians are subjected to all the "signs" and the statement is made "then Egypt will know that I am the Lord," [New English Bible. Exodus 7:5] no converts result. Once the Israelites got to the promised land, annihilating people is mentioned any number of times, converting them is never mentioned. Intermarriage is prohibited and then strangely, is allowed. As we have noted earlier in Ezra, intermarriage with non Israelites was considered the ultimate offense to God, the "holy race was contaminated." The "wives and their brood" were dismissed.

In the Book of Kings we read another story, we see another of many examples indicating a total absence of intention to convert non Israelites into becoming Israelites. Ahab was the King of Israel. Elijah accuses him of "forsaking the commandments of the Lord and following a god of the Gentiles by the name of Baal." [New English Bible. 1st Kings 18:18] This time the solution is not a horrific slaughter of wayward Israelites. This time Elijah proposed a very dramatic test, a face off, between himself with his Israelite God, against 450 prophets of Baal with their god. The 450 prophets of Baal, prepare a huge altar and put up a bull to be sacrificed. But no fire was to be lit. The test consisted of the 450 prophets of Baal praying to Baal to validate his reality by lighting the fire of their altar. This was to be followed by Elijah praying for fire to come down to his Israelite altar from his Israelite Lord God Jehovah. The story is so well written and dramatic that we will quote it. "Then Elijah said to the prophets of Baal, 'Choose one of the bulls and offer it first, for there are more of you; invoke your god by name, but do not set fire to the wood.' So they took the bull provided for them and offered it, and they invoked Baal by name from morning until noon, crying, 'Baal, Baal, answer us'; but there was no sound, no answer. They danced wildly beside the altar they had set up. At midday, Elijah mocked them: 'Call louder, for he is a god, it may be he is deep in thought, or engaged, or on a journey; or he may have gone to sleep and must be woken up.' They cried still louder and, as was their custom, gashed themselves with swords and spears until the blood ran. All afternoon they raved and ranted till the hour of the regular sacrifice, but still there was no sound, no answer, no sign of attention.

Then Elijah said to all the people, 'Come here to me.' They all came, and he repaired the altar of the Lord which had been torn down. He took twelve stones, one for each tribe of the sons of Jacob, the man named Israel by the word of the Lord. With these stones he built an altar in the name of the Lord; he dug a trench round it big enough to hold two measures of seed; he arranged the wood, cut up the bull and laid it on the wood. Then he said, 'Fill four jars with water and pour it on the whole-offering and on the wood.' They did so, and he said, 'Do it again.' They did it again, and he said, 'Do it a third time.' They did it a third time, and the water ran all round the altar and even filled the trench. At the hour of the regular sacrifice the prophet Elijah came forward and said, 'Lord God of Abraham, of Isaac, and of Israel, let it be known today that thou art God in Israel and that I am thy servant and have done all these things at thy command. Answer me, O Lord, answer me and let this people know that thou, Lord, art God.' … Then the fire of the Lord fell. It consumed the whole-offering, the wood, the stones, and the earth, and licked up the water in the trench. When all the people saw it, they fell prostrate and cried, 'The Lord is God, the Lord is God.' " [New English Bible. 1st Kings 18:25-39]

Of course, the god Baal fails miserably and Jehovah passes the test with flying colors. If we credit the prophets of Baal with any humanity and intelligence, and drive to life, this was a wonderful opportunity to convert at least some of those prophets. But this was not to happen. The purpose of the exercise was not to convert any gentiles. The purpose was to shore up the weak faith of the Israelites in their God. The opportunity to convert was not wished or intended and was wasted. The moment of increased faith on the part of the Israelites was put to work by Elijah by ordering his faith energized Israelites to "seize the prophets of Baal. Let not one of them escape." Elijah then brought them down to the brook Kishon and "there he slit their throats' [New American Bible. 1st Kings 18:40] It was never Elijah's intention to convert any of them.

One can speculate what response Elijah might have given if he had been asked why not convert these sons or prophets of Baal into sons of Abraham. I have no doubt that he would have been shocked by the heresy inherent in the question. No one can be changed or converted into an Israelite or son of Abraham. You can only be born a son of Abraham with that direct blood descent from the three great holy ancestors. And only, if you are a son of Abraham, can you be a member of the chosen people. The fate of the 450 Baal worshippers, none of them sons of Abraham, is not subject to speculation. All lay dead by the Kishon brook.

We have seen repeatedly the number one priority of the Israelite God: you must never worship other gods. The uncontrollable resulting rage invariably involved bloodshed. When the gentile wives were dismissed [Ezra] the "abominable practices" of these women was frequently mentioned. What exactly were these abominable practices? Are any pictures provided of the life and culture of these people? How really different was their culture? Are gods by different names actually different? Are these people not beset by exactly the same problems that the chosen people endured? Given that the chosen people strayed from the path, they were in consequence punished by their God with barren women (it seems at that time men never had low sperm counts), famines, pestilence, defeat and enslavement.

It is, of course, well known that these "punishments" are the common fate of mankind all across this globe. Even on the fully secluded Easter Island these curses presented themselves. But it remained largely impossible for the Israelites to find this common ground. We are chosen, they are not. And their leaders were very quick to point out the intense jealousy of Jehovah. There was no crossing, no rapprochement across these cultural, theological, and racial divides. David refers to Goliath as an uncircumcised Philistine. David is of the chosen people, Goliath is of the rejected people. Never the twain shall meet! Only in Job do we read anything in the Bible that suggests a huge expanse of common ground between the Israelites and the Gentiles.

"Why do the wicked gentiles enjoy long life, hale in old age, are great and powerful? They live to see their children settled, their kinsfolk and descendants flourishing; their families are secure and safe; the rod of God's justice does not reach them. Their bull mounts and fails not of its purpose; their cow calves and does not miscarry. Their children like lambs run out to play, and their little ones skip and dance; they rejoice with tambourine and harp and make merry to the sound of the flute. Their lives close in prosperity, and they go down to Sheol in peace. To God they say, 'Leave us alone; we do not want to know your ways. What is the Almighty that we should worship Him, or what should we gain by seeking his favor?" [New English Bible. Job 21:7-15]

The gentiles also have babies, raise their children and hope for continued progeny. The gentiles also have their flocks and fields. They also make music and dance and enjoy their prosperity. But even with all this common ground, it proved impossible for the Israelites to advance to the level of reduced animosity. The chosen remained the chosen ones.

Proceeding to Esdras in the Apocrypha, we read firstly a review and vindication of God's law forbidding the holy race from intermingling with the alien population. The chosen ones are not to contaminate their holy race. Expelling [New English Bible. 1 Esdras 8:94] those alien wives along with their "brood" is stated to be in accordance with God's judgment. Esdras then goes on to the "mystery of human destiny" and launches into a deep philosophical inquiry. He poses questions that others avoid for fear of the answers that may follow. If most people suffer here on earth and then go on to suffer interminably in the afterlife, why create those people in the first place? If God has chosen his people, and they follow his commands, imperfectly but better than any heathen nation, why is it that the heathen nations are allowed to defeat and enslave his chosen people? "I said to myself: 'Perhaps those in Babylon lead better lives, and this is why they have conquered Zion.' But when I arrived here, I have seen many evil doers with my own eyes. My heart sank, because I saw how you tolerate sinners and spare the godless; how you have destroyed your own people, but protected your enemies. You have given no hint whatever to anyone how to understand your ways. Is Babylon more virtuous than Zion? Has any nation except Israel ever known you? What tribes have put their trust in your covenants as the tribes of Jacob have? But they have seen no reward, no fruit for their pains. I have traveled up and down among the nations, and have seen how they prosper, heedless though they are of your commandments. So weigh our sins in the balance against the sins of the rest of the world; and it will be clear which way the scale tips. Has there ever been a time when the inhabitants of the earth did not sin against you? Has any nation ever kept your commandments like Israel? You may find one man here, one there; but nowhere a whole nation.'" [New English Bible. 2 Esdras 3:28-36] Esdras appeals to the Lord for answers but is insulted instead. Esdras is asked to "weigh a pound of fire, measure a bushel of wind, or bring back a day that has passed." He is told "you cannot possibly understand the ways of the Most High with your small capacity." Esdras continues courageously into the zone of the politically incorrect. He says "Better never to have come into existence than to be born into a world of wickedness and suffering which we cannot explain" [New English Bible. 2 Esdras 4:12] That persuades the Lord to start answering Esdras' questions. The answers include some very unsettling references to the chosen versus the unchosen peoples. "I have recited the whole story of the creation, O Lord, because you have said you made this first world for our sake; and that all the rest of the nations descended from Adam are nothing; that they are no better than spittle, and, for all their numbers, no more than a drop from a bucket. And yet, O Lord, those nations which count for nothing are today ruling over us and devouring us; and we, your people, have been put into their power -- your people, whom you have called your first-born, your only son, your champion, and your best beloved. Was the world really made for us? Why, then, may we not take possession of our world? How much longer shall it be so?" [2 Esdras 6:55-59] It is more than a little harsh to state that all the rest of the nations (all aliens, heathens, or gentiles) descended from Adam are nothing, they are no better than spittle. It is more than a little disconcerting to read this and acknowledge that I am not among the chosen. I am among those that are no better than spittle. It was this context of the chosen people that formed the philosophical undergirding, the literary heritage and cultural certainties of Jesus Christ. We shall see the implication in the gospel's very shortly.

Esdras goes on. At the judgment "I shall have joy in the few who are saved, because it is they who have made my glory prevail, and through them that my name has been made known. But I shall not grieve for the many who are lost." [New English Bible. 2 Esdras 7:60-61] Thus the explanation for the plenitude of suffering in the world and in the hereafter is that it is irrelevant to those that count. For God and those that are saved, the suffering of the rest is not even an inconvenience. That suffering is as irrelevant to them as is the suffering of the victims, in a 20th century extermination camp, is to the soulless and heartless monsters fulfilling the purpose of the camp. Unfortunately this concept taken from Esdras in the Apocrypha is reincarnated later. It is but a preview of the yet to be developed Christian concept of heaven and hell. The few saved are in a state of equanimity, joy, peace and tranquility while within sight and hearing of the cries of agony of the many damned. Have the saved lost all inclination and capacity for compassion? Has Mother Teresa been lobotomized into a compassionless, tranquil resident of heaven? Perhaps the Almighty in his wisdom will draw a curtain between heaven and hell and blinker the minds of his saved souls. Thus the saved will be spared the sights and sounds from hell. Nor will they think about the interminable agony on the other side of the curtain. And God, in his righteous anger can continue the torture of the dammed forever without disturbing the joy and tranquility of his saved souls. The concept is sufficiently repugnant that many Christian theologians now reject the concept of hell. Others manage to view God's righteous anger and hellish torture as fully compatible with a loving, forgiving, perfect God.

We will now conclude Esdras with his vision and understanding of the original choice by God of his chosen people.

" ' My Lord, my Master,' I said, 'out of the forests of the earth, and all their trees, you have chosen one plot; and out of all the flowers in the whole world you have chosen one lily. From the depths of the sea you have filled one stream for yourself, and of all the cities ever built you have set Zion apart as your own. From all the birds that were created you have named one dove, and from all the animals that were fashioned you have taken one sheep. Out of all the countless nations, you have adopted one for your own, and to this chosen people you have given the law which all men have approved.' " Again, it is disconcerting to be made acutely aware that I (you?) am not a member of that select, advantaged small group, the "chosen" ones.

We will now proceed to the gospels taking special note of the chosen people in Christ's ministry. Christ was born an Israelite, a member of the tribe of Judah, one of the twelve sons of Jacob. The collective heritage of these people contained a central and pervasive theme: they were the chosen people. We will have a predisposition to hope for less emphasis on and less privilege for the chosen peoples and greater acceptance of the previously non chosen peoples, the Gentiles. They also, we hope, will be within the reach of the saving message, that they will be worthy of sympathy and effort and that their grief and suffering will be taken note of.

The three wise men are among the first to take note of Christ's arrival. It is through them that King Herod hears of the birth of a child, destined to be the King of the Jews. He is alarmed to hear that a potential competitor to the kingship has arrived. Herod seeks information on this Messiah from the chief priests and teachers of the law. They inform him. He will be born in Bethlehem; he will be a leader who will be like a shepherd for my people Israel. [New English Bible. Matthew 2:6] Our immediate hopes are dashed. Does "my people Israel" include the Gentiles? Shortly after comes the story of the Roman centurion who approached Christ on behalf of his servant who is lying sick in terrible pain at home. Christ responds that he will "go and heal him". The centurion says, you need not come to my home, just give the order and my servant will be healed. Christ is utterly astonished at that level of faith from a non Israeli. And we are overjoyed to read Christs' next statement "Many will come from East and West and will sit at the table with Abraham, Isaac, and Jacob in the kingdom of heaven." [New English Bible. Matthew 8:11] We owe a debt of gratitude to the centurion for his level of faith resulting in a momentous promise from Christ. Perhaps, the "chosen" status of the Israelites is now less overpowering, perhaps the Gentiles are now part of the target audience. However, by Matthew 15:24 the dark cloud reappears over the Gentiles. A Canaanite woman approaches Jesus and his entourage shouting "Lord, son of David, have pity on me. My daughter is full of demons." Jesus does not say a word. This woman is not lacking in faith, but Christ seems to lack sympathy and compassion for this non-chosen woman. But she continues, undeterred, shouting and following along. The disciples, also lacking any trace of concern for her, tell Jesus to send her away. Christ now goes from saying nothing to her to stating "I was sent only to the people of Israel." Where do Gentiles fit in? Is God's plan for Christ exclusively for the chosen people? Has he forgotten the centurion episode? The woman continues undeterred. Now Christ states, "It isn't right to take food away from the children and feed it to the dogs" [Matthew 15:26] Who are the children? They are of course his chosen ones. Who are the dogs? How can it be that Christ himself used this pejorative put down for Gentiles commonly used by the Israelites? After Christ described Gentiles as dogs, the Canaanite woman abjectly reminds Christ that occasionally crumbs might fall from the children's table, crumbs a dog might eat. To Christ's credit, he finally yields. He says, "That's true. You may go now. The demon has left your daughter."

But the damage is done. "I was sent only for the people of Israel" is a difficult statement to re-interpret. The Gentiles have been left out of God's plan. The plan is exclusively there for the chosen ones. Contrast the difference. We have seen how the Canaanite woman fared. In Luke, 13:10-17, we read of an Israelite woman, a member of the family of Abraham. She had been crippled for eighteen years; completely bent over. When Jesus saw her, her called her over to himself and stated "You are now well." Was her treatment different from that which the Canaanite received? Luke continues with a very mixed message. The first chapter of Luke makes it very clear that the heritage of the chosen people is very much intact. Jesus is to become a king, just like King David, and rule the people of Israel forever. This curious promise, made by the angel Gabriel to Mary, raises more questions than answers. We know of King David's harem, his consummate military skill, his escapades with Bathsheba, his presentation of 200 Philistine foreskins to King Saul, and his final death, on his bed, of old age with Abishag by his side. How will Jesus be king of the Israelites "just like his ancestor David was"? But, through all of these questions, the status of the chosen ones is not a question. However, in the next chapter Luke is a little more open to the Gentiles. Simeon, a righteous and devout man, waiting for God to save the people of Israel, was in the temple when Mary and Joseph arrived with their newborn to dedicate him to the Lord. The holy spirit informed Simeon that this baby was the anointed one, the Messiah. He took up the baby Jesus in his arms. Then Simeon states that this baby will become "a light for revelation to the Gentiles," and a source of "praise and glory to your people Israel" [KJV Amplified Holy Bible. Luke 2:32] Once again we can hope, contradictory statements notwithstanding, that Christ's plan does include the Gentiles.

However, our hope is to be dimmed again. Peter asks Christ what rewards the disciples will get for having "left everything" to follow him. Christ's answer: "You will sit on twelve thrones to judge the twelve tribes of Israel" [Matthew 19:28] It is painful to note the complete exclusion of the Gentiles. But worse is to follow. In the tenth chapter of Matthew, Christ gives his instructions to the twelve apostles. His first instruction to them is:

- Stay away from the Gentiles [Bible for Today's Family]

OR

- Do not take the road to the Gentile lands. [New English Bible]

OR

- Go nowhere among the Gentiles. [KJV Amplified Holy Bible]

OR

- Do not make your way to the Gentile territory. [New Jerusalem Bible]

It makes no difference which Bible or which translation we encounter. We have the direct unequivocal statement from Christ: Do not go to the Gentiles. This statement is of course in complete accord with his earlier statement: "I was sent only for the people of Israel". His instructions go on: Do not go to the Samaritans. These people, like the Gentiles, despite their very close ties to the Israelites, are also to be excluded. The final instruction:

Go only to the people of Israel. Again, these three statements are difficult if not impossible to reinterpret into something more palatable. These are not spur of the moment declamations brought on by demonstrations of superior faith or lack of faith by any individual or group. These three statements are carefully considered policy statements given in the absence of distorting, frustrating or even exhilarating momentary circumstances. Christ's mind was clear. And the meaning was and is clear.

His three statements were so clear and so damaging to the prospects of Gentiles that you will never hear them as the focal point, or even side issue in any sermon. There is of course a lovely substitute homily theme quotation. It comes from the end of each of the first three gospels. It is given in its clearest form by Mark. "Go and preach the good news to everyone in the world. He that believeth and is baptized shall be saved." [Luke 16:15-16] What happened to "Do not go to the Gentiles?" We have here a complete reversal and we are left pondering why. What happened to Christ to effect such a monumental shift? Instead of focusing on one small tribe, his gospel is now to reach everyone? Christ's new position as we all know came about after his crucifixion and resurrection. Did the crucifixion change Christ's opinion on the Gentiles? Would his instructions now read "Do go to the Gentiles" and, of course, the Samaritans too?" It is difficult to explain a change of mind for an all knowing deity. The new message from Christ is cast under a shadow by what immediately follows the previous quotation. "Everyone who believes will be able to do wonderful things. By using my name they will force out demons, they will have the gift of speaking in tongues. They will handle snakes and drink poison and will not be hurt; "and the sick on whom they lay their hands will recover. … The Lord was with them and the miracles they worked proved that their message was true." [Mark 16:17-19] What a remarkably easy way to distinguish between the true and the false message and messengers! Speaking in tongues is easy. But handling poisonous snakes and drinking poison? In some back waters of the southern U.S. sects do exist that take these promises seriously. But in mainstream Christian thought these promises have long been discarded. No one would dream of handling snakes or drinking poison. And the laying on of hands is permissible only after the medical doctors have completed their job. So this part has been swept aside, but the quotation just before it has been made the cornerstone of Christian evangelism. Some parts are chosen, and others are rejected. How can this be done if all of the Holy Bible is inspired by the Holy Ghost, authorized by Christ and validated by God?

Any attempt to understand and explain this remarkable about-face immediately veers off into the extremely uncomfortable area of apostasy. We are to believe that Christ rose from the dead. In Mathew, Jesus appeared in Galilee to his eleven disciples but some of them doubted. In Mark, the expression "would not believe" occurs twice. Jesus appears in one form to Mary Magdalene and in another form to two disciples. In Luke, Jesus appeared to two disciples and but they do not recognize him. He walks with them from Jerusalem to Emmaus, about seven miles. They talk and still no recognition. When they sit down for supper and Jesus blesses the bread, they finally recognize Jesus, at which point Jesus disappears. He appears to his disciples and this time they think Jesus is a ghost. Christ encourages them to touch Him to verify for themselves that He really is Jesus and not a replica ghost. In John, Jesus appears to Mary Magdalene but this time she doesn't recognize Him; she thinks this someone was the gardener. When Jesus says, "Mary" she finally recognizes Him. In contrast to Luke's version, Jesus now says "Don't touch me". A week later Jesus appears to His disciples and encourages Thomas to touch Him. Finally Jesus appears again to seven of his disciples who are out fishing. Incredibly they do not recognize Him.

The purpose of Christ in appearing after the crucifixion was to verify to His believers that he had actually risen from the dead. Without his resurrection the entire message would have died. Why then did Christ choose to appear in different forms? Why appear to some and not to others? Why appear in such a form that his closest friends cannot recognize Him? Why encourage some to touch Him and forbid it to others? If His purpose was to demonstrate that He had risen from the dead, why appear in different forms and unrecognizable disguises? Why have four inspired accounts of His activities after His resurrection that are so different and contradictory that the heretical conclusion may be drawn that at least three of the accounts must be inaccurate? We will draw the conclusion that "Do not go to the Gentiles" was Christ's statement, contrariwise, the quotations about handling snakes and drinking poison: not Christ's statement. "Go and preach the good news to everyone in the world" was not Christ's statement. We will credit Christ with constancy and consistency, even if it comes at the expense of many preacher's favorite Biblical quotation. But this comes at the extreme expense of casting doubt on His resurrection. [The books Farewell to God, Charles Templeton, and A New Christianity for a New World, J. S. Spong, Chapter 6, detail the post resurrection contradictions].

We go to Acts. It begins with a very curious revision of the account of Judas' death given in Matthew. There a very remorseful Judas returns the thirty pieces of silver to the chief priests and hangs himself. Now, in the revision, Judas does not return the money, he buys some land. Then he dies a miraculous death; he fell into the field that he had purchased and his body burst open and his guts spilled out. This is followed by the account of the Holy Spirit coming over the disciples including tongues of fire, the sound of a mighty wind and the miraculous instantaneous learning of foreign languages. It is noteworthy that this was in effect the second assignment of the Holy Spirit because Christ himself, when he appeared to his disciples, already conferred the Holy Spirit upon them. "Then he breathed on them and said 'Receive the Holy Spirit'" [John 20:22] It is also noteworthy that some of those that heard the disciples talking in their instantly gained foreign languages drew the conclusion that the disciples were drunk.

The account very quickly goes on to the topic of special interest, the chosen people. Luke does not appear to be aware of Christ's post-crucifixion statement: Go to … the whole world, nor in a clear way of Christ's earlier statement "Do not go to the Gentiles." But he is very much aware of the tradition of the "chosen people." The high priests continued in opposition to the Apostles. But in the course of their powerful preaching and many miracles, converts were made. Especially the many healing miracles brought large numbers of all kinds of people, all desperate for healing. Steven, Philip and Peter were renowned healers. Paul became a very famed miracle healer; it is reported that "people even took handkerchiefs and aprons that had touched Paul's body and they carried them to everyone who was sick. All of the sick people were healed." [Acts 19:12] Just as Christ had more than just the chosen people come to Him, now people of all backgrounds came to the apostles. Cornelius, a Roman captain, was one such person. Peter went to visit him, and had a vision (he was very hungry and fell asleep) rejecting all the Mosaic Law food rules. All that abominable stuff that the Gentiles ate was suddenly O.K.! Peter goes much farther, "You know that we Jews are not allowed to have anything to do with other people, … but God has shown me that you, a Gentile, are not unclean." [Acts 10:28] After listening to Cornelius, Peter says, "Now I am certain that God treats all people alike." The chosen people are no longer the chosen people! Prior to meeting with Cornelius, Peter subscribed fully to the Mosaic Law and the chosen people, but now things have changed. Peter launches into a major sermon and the Holy Spirit took hold of all his listeners including Gentiles. The Jews there were very surprised. In Acts 11:18, it is repeated again. "God has now let the Gentiles turn to him." Paul now takes special responsibility to preach the good news to the

Gentiles. He preached in Corinth and discovered an awkward fact: the Gentiles could easily be persuaded of the good news but the Jews could not. They "turned against him and insulted him." Paul then draws this amazing conclusion. He says to the Jews, "What ever happens to you will be your own fault. I am not to blame. From now on, I am going to preach to the Gentiles." [Acts 18:6] One has the impression that the chosen ones have been abandoned to become the unchosen ones.

Why this level of resistance from the Jews? The book Judaism and Christianity by Trude Weiss-Rosmarin, is highly recommended for a complete answer. It will be sufficient here to mention the following. For the followers of the Mosaic Law, the followers of the God of Abraham, Isaac and Jacob, it proved to be impossible to give up the concept of being the chosen people. How can God make unequivocal promises to hold for all time and then do an about-face? How many times had they sinned before, but even in exile, they remained the chosen ones? If God were to have such a monumental change of heart, what's next? Does the Old Testament carry any value if the promise to be the God of his chosen people is abrogated and nullified? Next, the Jews, in particular their, high priests, were not satisfied with Christ's behavior. It was and is a time honored Jewish law and tradition that you respect your mother and father. The Jews simply could not overlook Christ's disrespectful behavior to his mother. She comes to talk to him, and he refuses to see her. He goes on to indicate that he has found substitutes for his mother. At the wedding at Cana, Jesus affronts his mother: "Woman, your concerns are not my concerns. My time has not yet come." Then he undergoes an instant attitude adjustment and, without even an apology, his unspoken words become "your concerns are my concerns, and yes, my time has come." Jesus is told, by recently persuaded followers, "Let us bury our dead first" and Jesus responds "Let the dead bury the dead." This constitutes the ultimate disrespect for the dead. To not properly bury the dead, without full attention to ritual requirements, was unthinkable. Just let the corpse attract scavengers and finally decompose and rot!? And Jesus' message about loving your enemies was regarded as outright insanity by the Jews. Where does it leave Judiths decapitation of Holophernes? Where does it leave the annihilation of the people who occupied the promised land? Where does it leave the concept of God the warrior? When evil people come to take your land and kill your family, a Jew has an obligation to defend, to the best of his ability, with the assistance of God. It is noteworthy that all countries of the world, lead by Christians or otherwise, consider it their sacred duty to defend their territory and people. Finally, the Jews had it firmly fixed in their theological traditions that the path to atonement came by one method, genuine repentance. "Repent ye!" was the famous call from John the Baptist. There is no doubt that repentance was both the necessary and sufficient condition for atonement. Paul introduced the concept of substitutionary atonement or sacrifice. A totally barbaric torture of an innocent lamb, Jesus, now became a necessary part of atonement. To the Jews, punishing an innocent party as a substitute for the guilty party was and is totally repugnant. Esdras makes it perfectly clear. "A father cannot send his son in his place, nor a son his father, a master his slave, nor a man his best friend to be ill for him, or sleep or eat or be cured for him. In the same way no one shall ever ask pardon for another, every individual will be held responsible for his own wickedness." [New English Bible. 2 Esdreas 7:105] In exactly the same way, when Moses offers to substitute himself for punishment for the guilty Israelites, God forbids the substitution. The Lord answered Moses "It is the man who has sinned against me that I will blot out of my book." [Exodus 32:31-33] The penalty must be paid by the guilty party. Sacrificing a perfectly innocent Jesus for the transgressions of sinners is just such a substitution. This is irreconcilable with Jewish ethics.

It is clear that when Paul's message fell on deaf ears among the Jews, and on fertile ground among Gentiles, he was strongly motivated to direct his efforts to the fertile ground. Once that step had been taken, it still remained a difficult revision to give up that very deeply ingrained concept of the chosen people. Not just do the Jews reject Paul's message, but they start resisting actively. They said Paul "goes around everywhere saying bad things about our nation and about the Mosaic Law, and about this temple. He has even brought shame to this holy temple by bringing in Gentiles." [Bible for Today's Family. Acts 21:28] The boundary lines become more clear all the time. The Jews adhering aggressively to their precepts and Paul and all the apostles moving with painful reluctance from familiar and well-loved Jewish thought to the only people that will listen to their message, the Gentiles. Paul states it clearly in his letter to the Romans. Whereas God had his favorites, his chosen people, in the Old Testament, now, in the post gospel New Testament "God has no favorites." [Romans 2:11]

The apostles attempted to cling to the "no favorites" concept but it proved very difficult to erase their very clear literary heritage. When we get to Revelations, also called the Apocalypse, written by John, we see a complete reversal back to the chosen people concept. We have seen earlier how the 144,000 who alone have been ransomed from the whole earth, are exclusively male virgins "who have not defiled themselves with women"

[New Jerusalem Bible. Revelations 14:4] Now we will take special note of the fact that it is further specified that everyone of the 144,000 are members of the chosen people. They divide up as follows: 12,000 from the tribe of Judah; 12,000 from the tribe of Reuben, and so on, until all 12 sons of Jacob have been listed. Our math will confirm that 12,000 x 12 = 144,000. As we noted before, we then find that the given requirement of a mark on the forehead, for all the servants of God is not fully exclusive. People without the mark, we are told, may also enter the kingdom of heaven. Here the distinguishing mark appears to be simply a white robe. At best what we have is 144,000 virgin chosen people, males, along with multitudes of white robed people who along with the 144,000, are also ransomed from the earth. Thus we have contradictions. Did only 144,000 get ransomed from the whole earth or not? If these quotations leave us holding out hope for the Gentiles, we have more clear negative indicators. We are given a vision of Jerusalem, the holy city coming down out of heaven from God. "It had all the glory of God and glittered like some precious jewel of crystal clear diamond. Its wall was of great height and had twelve gates; at each of the twelve gates there was an angel and over the gates were written the names of the twelve tribes of Israel. ... The city walls stood on twelve foundation stones each of which bore the name of one of the twelve apostles of the Lamb" [New Jerusalem Bible. Revelations 21:11-14] At what gate should the Gentiles enter? We continue reading "The throne of God and of the Lamb shall be there and his servants shall worship him; they shall see him face to face and bear his name on their foreheads" [Revelations 22:3] We must again ask where the Gentiles fit in. Only the 144,000 have that required mark on their foreheads. As before in Revelations 9:4, only those with the marked forehead make it into the holy city. "But outside the city will be dogs, witches, immoral people, murderers, idol worshipers and everyone who loves to tell lies and do wrong." [Revelations 22:15] None of the rejected categories of people is surprising or puzzling except, of course, the first and second ones. Witches?! Dogs?! Witches first. We know that some women (men too) would like to be or pretend to be witches complete with Satanic powers. But we are perfectly certain that acquiring Satanic powers is impossible. Without Satanic powers, we do not have a witch, we have a deluded human being. Certainly it would be better to propose a cure for them instead of keeping them outside the holy city. Dogs?! What about cats and rats and elephants? A more serious inquiry shows a clear and dismaying answer. Students of the Bible and scholars knowledgeable in the languages of the original manuscripts know exactly what the word "dog" means. It was the very commonly used pejorative by which the Israelites meant Gentiles. Dogs will stay outside of the holy city.

# Chapter 3
# Faith: Sceptics Rejected?

**Sceptics Rejected?**

There are many definitions of faith. They include:

1) The many sided religious relationship into which the gospel calls people, that of trust in God through Christ.

2) The unqualified acceptance of and exclusive dependence on the mediation of the Son as alone securing the mercy of the Father.

3) A body of truths (example, The Apostles Creed)

4) An exercise of trust that works miracles or prompts the working of miracles.

These definitions come from Evangelical Dictionary of Theology, Second Edition, Walter A. Elwell, Baker Academic. We will focus on the fourth definition, the one that is derived directly from Christ. And in order to make the definition more workable, applicable and understandable, we will refine the definition into: a mental state of certainty with respect to the power and willingness of Christ to perform a miracle. We all know what a miracle is. But we will define it never-the-less. It is a suspension of the laws of nature allowing an event to transpire that would, under the normal rule of the laws of nature, have been impossible.

The first miracle that Christ performs happened at the wedding at Cana. His mother asks Him to consider the problem of the wine. There is no more wine. Despite Jesus' immediate negative response, He does involve Himself in his mother's request and changes 150 gallons of water into 150 gallons of wine. The laws of nature are very clear on the transubstantiation from water to wine: it is impossible. However, Jesus accomplishes this violation of the laws of nature with the greatest of ease. We are aware of the Roman Catholic miracle of The Transubstantiation of wine to the blood of Christ which occurs at every mass. However, it is also very clear that the wine, after the miracle has been proclaimed, [This is the blood of Christ] has not been altered in any way, it is still wine. One cannot get drunk from drinking blood, but, as has been demonstrated countless times, it is easy to get drunk from consecrated wine. Here we have a miracle that is not a miracle because no law of nature has been violated. Anyone can understand that wine staying wine from one moment to the next is the law of nature. At the wedding at Cana, we are to believe that an actual miracle happened. We recognize further that Jesus did not raise the faith requirement in advance of performing this miracle. Certainly the "man in charge" and also the drinking wedding guests were not required to give evidence of faith.

The second miracle was also certainly a miracle. By the laws of nature a man does not recover from a serious disease from one moment to the next.

However, the faith requirement is set out much more clearly. In John's gospel we read the official's request followed by Jesus' rebuke, "you won't have faith unless you see miracles and wonders". Clearly the official, who has probably seen no miracles prior to this point in time, is found lacking in faith. But he goes on, "Please come before my son dies" Clearly the official lacks faith at the point that he is convinced that death is final. Jesus then gives the word that 'your son will live' followed by the statement that the official believes Jesus. In the account by Matthew, the official changes into an army officer and the official's son changes into the officer's servant. After making his request, the officer insists that Jesus need not come to his home to effect the healing miracle. This causes Jesus to comment "I've never found anyone with this much faith". Thus we see an indication from Christ that people of faith differ in the degree of that faith. That degree of faith we will understand as being the degree of certainty or conversely, the degree of absence of doubt concerning the power and willingness of Christ to perform the requested miracle. Jesus concludes this miracle with the important words "Your faith has made it happen." We conclude that in the absence of faith the miracle would not have happened.

Next we see a woman, who had been bleeding for twelve years, following Jesus. By now many people had been healed by Jesus. Many people had been brought to Jesus and He "healed everyone who was sick." [Bible for Today's Family. Matthew 8:16] The woman demonstrated faith by saying to herself "If I can just touch His clothes, I will get well." Jesus turns to her and says "Don't worry. You are now well because of your faith."

The next miracle is his first one reversing the finality death. A Jewish official requests of Jesus that he come to his home and place his hand on his daughter to bring her back to life. Unlike the army officer, he deems it necessary for Jesus to come in person to his home to perform this miracle. He arrives at the official's home and orders the mourners and musicians to leave saying "The little girl is not dead, she is just asleep." Then follows an astonishing demonstration of lack of faith, and even respect. "Everyone started laughing at Jesus" [Bible for Today's Family. Matthew 9:24] OR "And they laughed and jeered at Him." [KJV Amplified Holy Bible. Matthew 9:24]

Despite this highly irreverent and insulting demonstration of the lack of faith, Jesus performs this miracle anyway. The dead girl, in complete violation of the laws of nature, starts breathing and with Jesus holding her hand and helping her, she gets up. After the father of the dead girl has been admonished by Christ "Don't worry, just have faith," we are left with the impression that Jairus' faith passed the test. That is, Jairus was absolutely certain that Jesus would raise his daughter back to life. However, the facts point to the opposite. The people there with Jesus expected the dead girl to remain dead and when the fully unexpected did happen "Everyone was greatly surprised" [Bible for Today's Family. Mark 5:42] After completing the miracle, Jesus ordered them "not to tell anyone what had happened" [Luke]. However, these people again, demonstrating a lack of faith and respect, chose to ignore Christ's order. They spread the word such that the "fame hereof went abroad into all that country" [KJV Amplified Holy Bible. Matthew 9:26] It is disconcerting to read only four verses later that two blind men having been tested for their level of faith, having been healed of their blindness, and having been told because of your faith you are healed, also choose to contravene Christ's command. "Jesus strictly warned them not to tell anyone about Him. But they left and talked about Him to everyone in that part of the country." [Matthew 9:30-31] Again in Matthew 17:9, Jesus warns His disciples "not to tell anyone …"

Why is faith considered a necessary ingredient for a miracle to happen? Is Christ's power to perform a miracle somehow curtailed by the lack of faith? Is not a miracle the best way to produce faith? John puts it the most clearly: "Many people put their faith in Jesus because they saw Him work miracles" [Bible for Today's Family. John 2:23] Thus we have very troubling questions. Before addressing these questions we need to consider just a few more events. In Matthew 17 we read of a man whose son has demon induced epilepsy. His disciples had tried to cure the boy but could not. Jesus reacts with anger. He accuses them of stubborness and lack of faith. "How much longer must I be with you? Why do I have to put up with you?" Then Jesus spoke sternly to the demon and the boy was healed. But His disciples, disappointed by their inability to exorcise the demon, ask Him "Why couldn't we force out the demon?" This time Christ emphasizes the shortcomings of His own disciples: "It is because you don't have enough faith! But I can promise you this. If you had faith no larger than a mustard seed, you could tell this mountain to move from here to there. And it would. Everything would be possible for you." [Matthew 17:20-21] In Mark, Jesus' answer to his disciples is changed. Here his disciples are not upbraided for their lack of faith. Here Jesus tells them "Only prayer can force out that kind of demon."

In Matthew 21 Jesus sees a fig tree, and being hungry and expecting to find figs in the tree, he approaches the tree. Strangely, Jesus was wrong. How can Jesus be wrong? The tree had no fruit whatever. He finds that the tree had only leaves. Jesus becomes very angry and curses the tree: "You will never again grow any fruit!" Right then the fig tree dries up. Jesus' anger is hard to explain. It is even harder to explain when in Mark's version of the story [Mark 11] it is pointed out that it was not the season for figs. Does a rational person become upset or even angry with a plant for not bearing fruit when it is out of season? How do we describe a person filled with anger at any fruit tree for not bearing fruit, when just a few weeks earlier it did bear fruit when it was the right season to bear fruit? However, our main attention will go to Christ's next words. The disciples are astonished at the rapid effect of Jesus' curse on the fig tree. It dried up immediately. The astonished disciples are told by Jesus: "If you have faith in God and don't doubt, you can tell this mountain to get up and jump into the sea, and it will. Everything you ask for in prayer will be yours if only you have faith." [Bible for Today's Family. Mark 11:22-24] This promise of great power on the basis of absolute certainty, that is faith, and the complete absence of doubt, is reiterated a third time in Luke. After the apostles have requested "Make our faith stronger" Jesus says "If you had faith no bigger than a tiny mustard seed you could tell this mulberry tree to pull itself up, roots and all, and to plant itself in the ocean. And it would!" [Bible for Today's Family. Luke 17:6]

What a glorious promise of power from Christ. But move mountains? Uproot trees and plant them in the ocean? How did Christ come up with these examples? At least initially everyone understood this power promised by Jesus would provide an escape from the standard scourges of mankind. Famine, disease, pests, natural disasters, crime and war, all these are now subject to the power conferred by Christ to his people. If a famine threatens we need only think of His miracle where He fed 5000 men plus women and children with only five small loaves of bread and two fish [Luke 9:13]. If there is disease we need only recall Jesus' answer to John the Baptist's question "Are you the one?" [Luke 7] His answer was "Tell John what you have seen and heard, blind people are now able to see, the lame can walk. People who have leprosy are being healed, the deaf can hear. The dead are raised to life." These powers, including raising the dead back to life, have now been conferred upon His people. But the sceptics are the first to notice, but even the untutored masses quickly follow up: there is a condition. You will have these powers only if you have faith. The masses are encouraged when they read "If you had faith no bigger than a tiny mustard seed ..." They find themselves hoping that they do have that requisite tiny mustard seed of faith. The desperate realization is of course that without the requisite tiny mustard seed of faith, "no mountains will move", their prayer at the bedside of their fatally sick child will not be answered; the famine advances and their prayers for bread and fish will go unanswered. For the sceptic the problem is far more serious. She realizes that the sceptic by definition will not have the required level of faith. Further she will know with absolute certainty that many among the untutored masses, people with more than a tiny mustard seed of faith, have died of famine and/or disease. And raising people from the dead? It is one thing to believe in life after death. It is quite another to believe that a person that has died can be raised back to earthly life. Thus the untutored masses have vague apprehensions that the promise may not be as good as it first sounded. To the sceptic the promise is quickly becoming an incredibly callous sham.

The Irish promise a pot of gold at the end of the rainbow. Children believe this and run about in the meadows after a thundershower trying to get to the end of the rainbow. Maybe the pot of gold is there. But the condition to locate it cannot be fulfilled. If you are promised a bank account full of money that you can access if you can find where it is, the promise is immediately perceived as being hollow. Advertisements for lottos promise huge amounts of money on two conditions. Firstly, you must have a ticket and secondly you must have the right lucky numbers. An elementary course in Statistics will tell you what your chance of winning, and conversely of loosing, is. It is encouraging to know with absolute certainty that despite the odds, a very, very few people will and have won. Back to the promise Christ made. How many among the nine million Ukrainians that were starved to death by the communists in Moscow were faithful, prayerful Christians? Did they offer up prayers for bread and fish? Or is there some fine print in Christ's promise that made it impossible to intervene? Surely some people would have had the requisite tiny mustard seed of faith to access these powers. Did Mother Theresa have sufficient faith? Does the Roman Catholic Pope have sufficient faith? Perhaps Martin Luther or Billy Graham or some of the very loud evangelists we see on T.V.?

From our present perspective we see faith healing of disease has fallen into total disrepute. So many charlatans have enriched themselves in the past by abusing those of childish or childlike faith that T.V. documentaries have been presented showing the fraud they utilized. A picture of Christ is a basic minimum.

Then the standard prompts. Do you have faith? Do you believe that Christ/God wishes to heal you? Do you have faith that a miracle for you is about to happen? Of course at some point reality does inject itself into this situation. These charlatans do not work for free. The T.V. evangelists proclaim "We expect a miracle". And yet it is well known that when a limp is miraculously healed in front of 5000 believers, no one, at that moment, will come forward to question the reality of that miracle. How could anyone, at that moment, affront the evangelist, the 5000 believers and God who just performed the wonderful miracle? And yet, when at some later date, you see the girl whose limp was previously healed, walking toward her church, heavy doubts assail you. Of course, I do recognize her, for sure. But, didn't she get healed of her limp? Evidently not, because she is now in need of a further miracle. Because she is now limping even worse than before the first miracle.

"The blind people are now able to see." Faith healing for eye problems does not seem to happen at all anymore. Very complicated technology and surgical skills are employed, for example, to remove cataracts. The old clouded lens is replaced by a new artificial lens with absolutely miraculous effect. We note here the word miraculous in no way implies a violation of the laws of nature. It now means that as a consequence of intense long term chemistry, biology, physics, etc. with thousands of tests, to unravel the laws of nature, we can now accomplish astounding things entirely within the laws of nature.

"The dead are raised to life" Here the answer is categorical. No way! Absolutely not. Again with high tech modern methods we can prolong life and we can bring back people, sometimes, from the very brink of death. But after you have been certified dead and the life insurance benefit has been paid, you cannot be raised back to life. In the case of fraudulent insurance claims, absolutely no one even entertains the thought that the dead person was raised back to life.

Thus the sceptic and even the untutored masses now have very serious misgivings about Christ's promises. Is the promise as empty as the pot of gold at the end of the rainbow? But the sceptic now proposes an analysis of Christ's promises. He proposes that we test the promise. Christ seems to have been ready for this challenge. Instead of saying, go ahead, God will easily pass any test of His commitment to stand by any promise he ever made, we receive an utterly devastating body blow. We are not allowed to test God in any way. We are given the great promises but when we have the unbelievers or believers assembled, and we wish to demonstrate God's power, we might ask God to heal an Aids victim. But we are not allowed to ask it because it would constitute a test. And we know the quotation "Don't try to test the Lord your God" [Matthew 4:7] When does a faithful, prayful request to God become a test of God? What do we think of a person who claims to be honest and caring and then adds "but don't ever test me?" Does it matter one iota if a mother and father pray for healing for their dying child if the request is refused because they lack that tiny seed of faith or because God senses that their prayer might constitute a test? In either case, the child dies.

It is interesting to note that in the Old Testament, God did not object to being deliberately tested. We have noted previously the vastly interesting story contained in 1 Kings 18. Elijah challenges the 450 prophets of Baal to a face-off between his God, the Lord God of the Israelites, against their god Baal. Huge altars are prepared but would remain unlit by the hand of man. The fire was to be lit by their respective God. Baal does not pass the test. Despite quiet prayers, loud prayers, wild dancing, self flagellation, gashing, ranting and raving, Baal does not come through. Then it is Elijah's turn. Does God refuse to be tested? Of course not! Even after pouring buckets and buckets and buckets (yes, three times) of water over everything on Elijah's altar, God responds after only the first short request by Elijah "Lord God of Abraham, Isaac and Israel, let it be known today … ." Then the fire of the Lord fell. What a dramatic way to be tested and what a glorious way to pass that test. But that was in the Old Testament, Now the situation has been reversed. Tests are not allowed.

Yet another Old Testament quotation not just allows testing of God but encourages it. At the very end of the Old Testament we read in Malachi "Bring all the tithes into the storehouse that there may be food in My house, and <u>prove Me</u> now by it, says the Lord of Hosts, if I will not open the windows of heaven for you and pour out a blessing that there shall not be room enough to receive it." [<u>KJV Amplified Holy Bible</u>. Malachi 3:10] We see that God is encouraging us to test Him: pay your tithes, the full ten percent, and God will pass the test by blessing you generously. Why the momentous change in the New Testament?

Let us review the promises of miraculous powers made directly or indirectly or by implication by Christ to His followers:

1) "I tell you not to worry about your life. Don't worry about having something to eat, drink, or wear. Isn't life more than food or clothing? Look at the birds in the sky! They don't plant or harvest. They don't even store grain in barns. Yet your Father in heaven takes care of them. Aren't you worth more than birds." [<u>Bible for Today's Family</u>. Matthew 6:25-26]

2) "Don't worry and ask yourselves, 'Will we have anything to eat? Will we have anything to drink? Will we have any clothes to wear?" Only people who don't know God are always worrying about such things. Your

Father in heaven knows that you need all of these. But more than anything else, put God's work first and do what he wants. Then all the other things will be yours as well." [Bible for Today's Family. Matthew 6:31-33]

3) "Ask, and you receive. Search, and you will find. Knock, and the door will be opened for you. Everyone who asks will receive. Everyone who searches will find. And the door will be opened for everyone who knocks. Would any of you give your hungry child a stone, if the child asked for some bread? Would you give your child a snake if the child asked for a fish? As bad as you are you still know how to give good gifts to your children. But your heavenly Father is even more ready to give good things to people who ask." [Bible for Today's Family. Matthew 7:7-11]

4) "As you go, announce that the kingdom of heaven will soon be here. Heal the sick, raise the dead to life, heal people who have leprosy, and force out demons." [Bible for Today's Family. Matthew 10:7-8]

5) "Jesus answered 'Go and tell John what you have heard and seen. The blind are now able to see, and the lame can walk. People with leprosy are being healed, and the deaf can hear. The dead are raised to life, and the poor are hearing the good news.'" [Bible for Today's Family. Matthew 11:4-5]

6) "But they said, 'We have only five small loaves of bread and two fish.'" [Bible for Today's Family. Matthew 14:17]

"After everyone had eaten all they wanted, Jesus' disciples picked up twelve large baskets of leftovers. About five thousand men were there, not counting the women and children." [Bible for Today's Family. Matthew 14:20-21]

7) "But we don't want to cause trouble. So go cast a line into the lake and pull out the first fish you hook. Open its mouth and you will find a coin. Use it to pay your taxes and mine." [Bible for Today's Family. Matthew 17:27]

8) "I promise that when any two of you on earth agree about something you are praying for, my Father in heaven will do it for you." [Bible for Today's Family. Matthew 18:19]

9) "The disciples were shocked when they saw how quickly the tree had dried up. But Jesus said to them, 'If you have faith and don't doubt, I promise that you can do what I did to this tree. And you will be able to do even more. You can tell this mountain to get up and jump into the sea, and it will. If you have faith when you pray, you will be given whatever you ask for." [Bible for Today's Family. Matthew 21:20-22]

10) "Jesus replied, "Why do you say if you can? Anything is possible for someone who has faith!" [Bible for Today's Family. Mark 9:23]

11) "Jesus told him: You can be sure that anyone who gives up home or brothers or sisters or mother or father or children or land for me and for the good news will be rewarded. In this world they will be given a hundred times as many houses (!?) and brothers and sisters and mothers and children and pieces of land though they will also be mistreated. And in the world to come, they will have eternal life." [Bible for Today's Family. Mark 10:29-30]

12) Have faith in God! If you have faith in God and don't doubt, you can tell this mountain to get up and jump into the sea, and it will. Everything you ask for in prayer will be yours, if you only have faith." [Bible for Today's Family. Mark 11:22-24]

13) "Then he told them: Go and preach the good news to everyone in the world. Anyone who believes me and is baptized will be saved. But anyone who refuses to believe me will be condemned. Everyone who believes me will be able to do wonderful things. By using my name they will force out demons, and they will speak new languages. They will handle snakes and will drink poison and not be hurt. They will also heal sick people by placing their hands on them." [Bible for Today's Family. Mark 16:15-18]

14) "Then the disciples left and preached everywhere. The Lord was with them, and the miracles they worked proved that their message was true." [Bible for Today's Family. Mark 16:20]

15) "Jesus called together his twelve apostles and gave them complete power over all demons and diseases. Then he sent them to tell about God's kingdom and to heal the sick." [Bible for Today's Family. Luke 9:1-2]

16) "The apostles said to the Lord, "Make our faith stronger!" Jesus replied "If you have faith no bigger than a tiny mustard seed you could tell this mulberry tree to pull itself up,, roots and all, and to plant itself in the ocean. And it would!" [Bible for Today's Family. Luke 17:5-6]

17) "Jesus answered, "You can be sure that anyone who gives up home or wife or brothers or family or children because of God's kingdom will be given much more in this life. And in the future world they will have eternal life." [Bible for Today's Family. Luke 18:29-30]

18) "I tell you for certain that if you have faith in me, you will do the same things that I am doing. You will do even greater things, now that I am going back to the Father. Ask me, and I will do whatever you ask. This way the Son will bring honor to the Father. I will do whatever you ask me to do." [Bible for Today's Family. John 14:12-14]

19) "Stay joined to me and let my teachings become part of you. Then you can pray for whatever you want, and your prayer will be answered." [Bible for Today's Family. John 15:7]

20) "You did not choose me. I chose you and sent you out to produce fruit, the kind of fruit that will last. Then my Father will give you whatever you ask for in my name." [Bible for Today's Family. John 15:16-17]

21) "I tell you for certain that the Father will give you whatever you ask for in my name. You have not asked for anything in this way before, but now you must ask in my name. Then it will be given to you, so that you will be completely happy." [Bible for Today's Family. John 16:23-24]

22) "If you are sick, ask the church leaders to come and pray for you. Ask them to put olive oil on you in the name of the Lord. If you have faith when you pray for sick people, they will get well. The Lord will heal them and if they have sinned, he will forgive them. [Bible for Today's Family. James 5:14-15]

The promises are self explanatory. They are wonderful. They are glorious. But there are conditions attached to these promises: these powers will be accorded only to those people who have the necessary amount of faith, and secondly, the prayer request must be made in such a way that it will not be seen as a test by God. And finally, a very easy condition to satisfy: "You must ask in my name." [John 16:23-24]

Now we must review the promises and the attached conditions in the light of reality. The example of Lourdes comes to mind. In the year 1858, we are to believe that the Virgin Mary appeared to a peasant girl. Healing miracles started to happen. The word spread and thousands and then millions came each year to strengthen their faith and to pray for miraculous healings. Many miracles were reported, but the Vatican became concerned when reports came to them that many claimed faith healings were fraudulent. New rules were set in place to avoid the embarrassment of these fraudulent claims. Now miraculous healings were subject to a threefold test: 1) A professional medical diagnosis prior to a visit to Lourdes had to be in place. 2) Professional medical teams must have previously applied their skills fully and admit to failure, that is, no cure for the patient. 3) Professional medical doctors were required to verify, immediately after the visit to Lourdes, that a cure had actually been brought about.

With these curtailments in place, the miracles ceased almost completely. Indeed now the number of miracles at Lourdes matches the number of miracles in the hospitals run by our medical professionals. But in hospitals, they are not called miracles, they are called spontaneous remissions. We are aware, of course, of the "negative miracles" that also happen in our hospitals (and elsewhere). They are called spontaneous reinvigorations of the pathogenic organism. The patient must deal with the unexpected worsening of his condition. As of now, our scientific insights are insufficient to explain every time why some patients get better and others get worse. The overall conclusion is clear: faith healing is a highly suspect business. We know that faith healing is at least 99 percent expensive fraud. We are left wondering if faith healing as it is reported in the Bible is like faith healing at Lourdes. Was it fraudulent?

Before drawing any further conclusions we will once more review the testing of God as it is presented in the Old Testament. In Daniel, Bel and the Snake, Cyrus the Persian became the king. Daniel, an Israelite, was a confidant of the king, the most honored of all the king's friends. The Babylonian king believed in the god Bel. As evidence that Bel was actually a living god, the priests of Bel pointed out that each day a sacrifice of twelve bushels of fine flour, forty sheep, and fifty gallons of wine were left on the altar in front of Bel and by the morning of the next day, all the food would be gone, all consumed by Bel. One wonders if the very human god Bel, having eaten copiously, would not also be compelled to produce a daily divine bowel movement. Daniel proposed a test, not of his God, but of the Babylonian god. Daniel claimed that Bel was actually dead, clay inside and bronze outside, and as such could not eat anything. Amazingly, the king and the priests of Bel agreed to the test. It is generally agreed that any religion that allows itself to be tested is a weak and waning religion. Penalties are put in place. If Bel refuses to consume the food, the priests, their wives and children will be put to the sword, and if Bel does consume the food, Daniel will die for his blasphemy against Bel. Daniel and the king set out the food in front of Bel, and with no priests present, Daniel sifted ashes over the floor of the temple. Then, they sealed the temple door with the king's signet. The following morning the king and Daniel entered the temple and, sure enough, all the food was gone. But even the king could see all the footprints on the floor. A secret entrance to the temple was soon found. It was the priests with their families who had eaten all of the food. They were put to death. The test of Bel went clearly against Bel. What an astonishing application of the scientific method, and this, way back, in the Old Testament!

But the story continues. The Babylonians had a huge snake that they believed was a god. Once again Daniel proposes a test. The king agrees that if the snake is divine, it will not be easy to kill it. Daniel's test will be an attempt to kill the snake without sword or staff. The king gives Daniel the go ahead. Then Daniel took pitch and fat and hair. This he placed in the mouth of the seemingly tranquil snake. Contrary to all expectations, the snake ate it and then burst open and died. The test showed clearly, the snake was not divine.

Now the story takes a very different turn. The Babylonians begin to resent a king who has fallen under the influence of Daniel, a foreigner, to the point that he murdered their priests and killed the snake. Under pressure from the rabble, he turns Daniel over to them who throw him into a lion pit. With the lions ration of two sheep per day discontinued, they were sure the lions would get hungry enough to devour Daniel. But this was not to happen. The lions did not get hungry, but Daniel did. The God of the Israelites then bethought Himself what to do. The prophet Habakkuk was just then making a meat stew plus crumbled bread to take out to his harvesting crew to feed them. An angel was sent and Habakkuk, plus food, was transported to Babylon, all the way from Judea. The angel "took the prophet by the crown of his head, and carrying him by his hair he swept him off to Babylon … and put him down into the lion pit." [New English Bible. Daniel Bel and the Snake 36:37] Daniel was overjoyed to receive his lunch. The lions still were not hungry. Days later the king went to the pit to mourn for Daniel only to see him hale and hearty, in superb form. Now follows a thoroughly amazing lapse in the mind of the Persian king. Having had his deities tested twice it does not occur to him to demand to have it verified and revealed to him how the God of the Israelites had kept Daniel so well fed and watered. Exactly how did you obtain food? You say Habakkuk flew here with his harvest crew's food!? This I have to see for myself! You will stay where you are, in the lion pit, and I will stay where I am until we both see the angel carrying Habakkuk plus food and drink to you. Let's make this a test for your God just as we tested my gods. This of course was not to be. The story continues with the king pulling Daniel out of the pit, throwing the enemies of Daniel into the pit. The lions suddenly noticed they were very hungry and devoured the men immediately.

We have the previously listed powers. Why does Christ so extravagantly empower his followers to be able to uproot trees and move mountains when even the standard requests for food and healing of diseases are not to be realized? After many famines around the world with many unanswered prayers, how can we be expected to have no doubt, only solidly certain faith when it is our turn to face the misery of famine? How can I, having witnessed the prayers of immediate family at the bedside of a severely sick eight month old brother, maintain my faith when my brother did not survive? Is it not repugnantly and immorally callous to expect certainty and faith when we have evidence of others all around us whose prayers went unanswered? And when we get to raising people from death the evidence mounts right up to a 100 percent failure rate. No one, to the best of my knowledge, would even remotely consider raising the dead to life. Even to entertain the thought to bring a loved one back to life would be to invite insanity. The promises of power are thus empty. The unanswered questions leave Christ's message in severe doubt.

Add to this fact that often after performing a miracle, He would demand of the healed person not to tell anyone. Why? How can it be that when Christ knows that "people put their faith in Jesus because they saw Him work miracles", how can it then be that He would forbid them from spreading the word of His miraculous healing to anyone else? We know that the leadership of the Jews, the Teachers of the Laws, the Pharisees and the Saducees requested a sign or a miracle from Jesus many times. But instead of accommodating these sceptics with an immediate "of course," Jesus responds with anger. Indeed His anger ramps up so quickly that His intellectual faculties are temporarily disabled. "And He groaned and sighed deeply in His spirit and said, 'Why does this generation demand a sign? Positively I say to you, no sign shall be given to this generation'." [KJV Amplified. Mark 8:12] No sign for this generation? Has He forgotten the hundreds of signs already performed? Groaned and sighed? What was He thinking? Imagine yourself a young strong macho man hired as a labourer. You have just loaded five tons of gravel on a truck by shovel. You are sweating. The boss arrives, "Good work, but why are you resting on your shovel? Get to work on the five trucks lined up for you over there." You have a right to groan and sigh. You may be pardoned for considering going back to school. How tough, how draining is it for Christ to perform a miracle? Isn't the cost of a miracle to God or Christ something less than a dime a dozen? Even in the towns of Chorazin and Bethsaida, despite their lack of faith, Jesus performed many miracles [Matthew 11:20] to no effect. But it is Jesus' next statement that again astounds us: "If the miracles that took place in your towns had happened in Tyre and Sidon (and even Sodom) the people there would have turned to God." [Matthew 11:21] If miracles would have led to faith and salvation in those three towns, why was it not done? Call upon an angel or utilize a prophet. Do the signs and miracles! But it was not done. For lack of Christ's/God's willingness to perform the miracles, those people are "in for trouble". How can we reconcile a loving God with one who will not expend a miniscule amount of time and energy to perform those miracles? I do not know.

"You want a sign because you are evil" [Matthew 12:39] Why is Jesus so averse to the wisest and most learned among His fellow Jews who have the necessary experience, learning and judgment to realize that Israel (and other nations also) was full of fraudsters. Isn't it worthwhile to verify the real event or expose the hoax? Was Christ afraid that these learned people would discover Him to be a fraud? Why avoid a test if you can easily pass it? Jesus hated the sceptics, the Pharisees, Saducees and Teachers with such intensity that He expresses joy at the forthcoming damnation of those people: "At that time Jesus felt the joy that comes from the Holy Spirit and He said My father, Lord of heaven and earth, I am grateful that you have hidden these things from the wise and educated people and showed it to the ordinary people." [Luke 10:21] Again we are aghast. Has God actually intervened against the leaders of his chosen people? Has he ensured, by hiding these things from them, that they will surely go to hell? And Christ thanks God for this and feels joy in this context? The concept is too repugnant. We have reluctantly tried to accept God's hardening of Pharaoh's heart. Now we have an even harder time accepting God's deliberate "hiding these things." It cannot be. But Christ's words are there. What are our options?

The scientific method has achieved all of its glorious successes by virtue of its insistence on testing. When a particular compound is credited, by one team of scientists, as being an effective antibiotic, others will be invited to test it against the claims made. If another compound is heralded as effective for pain control for dental procedures, you can be certain it will be tested. Likewise, if our Global Positioning System is announced and tested, we can rest assured that our jet will come down over the right Hawaiian Island, directly over the right runway, despite clouds, fogs or darkness. Further we can fully trust in the total constancy of the laws of nature. It simply will not and cannot happen that the laws of electromagnetism will suddenly be altered halfway to our Hawaiian Island bringing us down prematurely in the Pacific. But science will forever suffer from the fact that its practitioners operate at an applied intellectual level that is totally inaccessible to others unless they are prepared to spend many years sharpening their intellectual grasp and reach. My own Sunday School question "How did this mountain get here?" was given the extremely complete and satisfying answer, "God put it there." This answer would receive a failing grade from any scientist. The Old Testament would have us believe that Joshua commanded the sun and moon to stand still in order to more effectively massacre and annihilate the Amorites. "So the sun stood still and the moon halted … " [Joshua 10:13] Many years later Galileo found fault with this astounding miracle. "It cannot be so" he stated. And the Holy Roman Catholic Church imposed incarceration and the threat of being burned at the stake, as they had done to countless others. Four hundred years later the Catholic Church apologized for what they did to Galileo. They conceded that Galileo, the scientist, was right and that the Bible account was erroneous, a myth. He did the same for the parting of the waters as the Israelites escaped. The waters did not part. And, mercifully, the most repugnant miraculous curse against the Egyptians, the killing of all their first borns: it did not happen.

It is the pattern here that we must recognize. Miracles happened on a daily basis when credulous and gullible people, encouraged by their leaders, allowed their imaginations unfettered scope. Testing to determine the validity or fraudulence of a particular miracle was discouraged or even threatened by torture and/or death if a finding of fraudulence might impact negatively on the established powers. Thus the churches persecution of many scientists. Where the foundation of a religion rests upon miracles that violate the laws of nature, it may be expected that this religion would strike back in fear and anger against those who would test those claims. Again the established pattern is very clear: the miraculous violations of the laws of nature disappear before the testing sceptic as the rabbits in the meadow scurry away when the fox arrives.

Let us now review in some detail the miracle of healed blindness given in the ninth chapter of John. Jesus passes a man who was born blind. His disciples raise a question that has instant resonance with us. "Rabbi, who sinned, this man or his parents that he should be born blind?" [KJV Amplified] A treasure trove or is it a Pandora's box of questions has been opened. So many babies are born with defects that run the gamut from light to onerous to fatal. Why does this happen? Jesus answers "It was not that this man or his parents sinned, but he was born blind in order that the workings of God should be manifested, displayed and illustrated in him." It requires a second reading to fully understand the astounding answer. He was born blind to create an opportunity to perform a sign or miracle! Do we have here a validation of the principle that the ends justify the means? The man may now suffer horribly from his blindness but in the end, it will manifest the workings of God. In Christ's mind it must have made sense. In the gospel the disciples are presented as being satisfied with Christ's answer. No more questions are forthcoming from them. But if we credit the disciples with even a tiny spark of intellectual capacity and curiosity we can immediately hear more questions gushing forth. Or was there intellectual straightjacketing? Were there questions raised but the writer of the gospel deleted them? We can surely speculate on what they would have asked next. What of those babies who were born blind who never had the good fortune of encountering you? And what of those whose congenital defects were so severe that they lived a short miserable, tortuorous life only to die prematurely? And, we might add, what of those babies born with "flipper" defects resulting from thalidomide, a medication to ease the discomforts of pregnancy, a medication released without sufficient testing? Is it possible that this suffering was caused by the sins of the baby? Was it caused by the sins of the parents? Are we to accept it as justice that the sins of ancestors will be visited, as grievous suffering, upon the newly arrived innocent infant? The thought of it makes one shudder. But the question has been raised in our minds. Why these defects at birth? And Jesus leaves the question weighing heavily on our minds with no hope for any kind of answer.

But the story goes on. With no faith requirements insisted upon Jesus proceeds with the astounding sign. He spat on the ground, mixed the dirt with the spittle and then applied this paste on the blind mans eyes. Then he told the still blind man to go to the Siloam pool and rinse the mud off his eyes. "He went his way and washed and came back seeing." So we have a profound violation of the laws of nature completed. Ophthalmologists are in complete agreement: The eyes and ophthalmic nerves of a person born blind will be totally atrophied within a few short months. The brain's processing capacity for electrical signals from the ophthalmic nerves will not be developed and therefore does not exist. Where such a miracle is presently claimed, ophthalmologists would reject it out of hand. Sorry, it cannot be, stop wasting our time. What of the miracle reported in John? Reality or hoax?

The Pharisees got involved. The miracle was studied. And the Pharisees found themselves in the uncomfortable role of the sceptic. They express the suspicion that this is not the man who was born blind. But the parents confirm: yes, the now seeing man is the one born to us years ago, blind. Again, perhaps due to intellectual straight-jacketing, the Pharisees are not reported as immediately pursuing the next logical course of action. Every country has its homes for the blind. It would have been the easiest thing in the world to procure another blind from birth person. Present that person to Christ to again manifest the workings of God. Perhaps, the unreported sequence of events was, as I have speculated, complete with anger from Christ about an evil generation demanding another sign. It remains clear that no sane religious leader of today would ever attempt the miracle of restoring sight to any blind from birth person.

Thus we have the extravagant empty empowering promises. We have the faith requirement; the no testing allowed provision and frequent admonition "Don't tell anyone about this miracle." And finally we have virulent hatred of Christ for the sceptic. He calls them the offspring, not of Abraham, but of the devil. he accuses them of behaving like their father, of lusting and murdering. And he thanks God for hiding these things from the wise and learned, that is, from the sceptics. And while he performed countless signs, for almost anyone, (sometimes he required faith and at other times no requirements), he would not for the sceptics. We know that the sceptics (ourselves included) would be vastly impressed and immediately moved to faith. But we are acutely aware that the childish or childlike can easily be deceived by a fraudulent miracle. Is it a sin to request that a miracle should be free of the stench of deception and fraud? Are we sure that Christ could easily have provided a genuine miracle for the Jewish leadership, the sceptics? We may be helped by answering "if he could have he should have, indeed, he would have had to, given his professed love of sinners. But he didn't. Jesus claimed that when he was in his hometown that he "could not work any miracles" [Mark 6:5] The all-powerful Christ/God could not!? Are we to believe both - that he is all-powerful and that he could not? The reason was too many faithless sceptics. We will dare to assume that under the skilled watchful eye of the sceptics, Christ fully realized that the miracles could not happen. The reason for Christ's insistence on no testing and no signs for the sceptics was because he realized, he knew full well, that laws of nature can't be trampled and trashed. Water to wine? With a sceptic invigilating? Not possible! Blind from birth restored to sight? Not possible! Now, or in the future or in the past. Only if the laws of nature change. And they will not.

Now it makes sense that Christ would try to prevent the spread of stories about His miracles. Think of all the people arriving, with heavy water jars, expecting a miracle with, of course, an immediate test to determine the quality of the wine! Others, with a higher degree of faith, would arrive with lighter empty water jars believing firmly that Christ could and would refill them with wine. And yet others, with an even higher degree of totally childlike faith, recalling the Roman army officer, would have left the empty water jars at home: of course, Christ can refill them at a distance. No need whatever to come to their homes! When Jesus said "Talitha koum!" and the twelve year old daughter of Jairus was raised to life, can you imagine the intensity of the excitement of everyone who found out? How many people would think of their recently or not so recently deceased loved one? At his next meeting we can see him surrounded by his faithful believers, each bringing the exhumed remains of loved ones; some dead only two days ago, some dead a year or more ago. His miracle would have been put to the test repeatedly and immediately with dire failures every time. No wonder Jesus ordered them not to tell anyone.

What of all the miracles to be seen any day on the many shows from the T.V. evangelists? We have seen the healed girl limping back. The typical miracle they perform is the religious charlatan's favorite miracle. In the extreme psychological frenzy that the evangelists engender in their audiences, the brains of many people become temporarily unhinged. Visions are seen. Reality is blurred. Super human efforts come with ease. The miracle seekers attempt with all the strength and concentration they can muster to believe that they have been healed. Will the evangelists attempt to heal a blind from birth person? No! Will they bring up a legless wheelchair believer to attempt a miraculous leg replacement? No! Will they bring a migraine sufferer to cure a headache? Yes! A wheelchair believer whose legs and back are very weak? Yes! And by a super human effort they will get up and prance about to the "Amens, glory halleluiahs, and sweet Jesuses" of the mob around them. Later in the quiet of their home, their legs and back will be in worse shape than before. There is nothing an evangelist and his crowd of believers hate more than a person trying to report a failed miracle. The assembled crowd is not there to have cold water dashed upon their desire to experience a glorious high, a sense of relief, a powerful certainty together with many other desperate believers. So if it didn't work last time, step forward with increased faith and we'll heal you again. Sceptics will either not come or they will remain silent. They may be escorted out. Thus the invariable silence at, or absence of sceptics at these evangelical rallies.

There is no lack of books and authors that take the point of view that miraculous violations of the laws of nature happen routinely. Typically such authors have the desperate motivation to validate the many miracles that form the central focus of their religion. They may also be motivated by the promise of financial success guaranteed when the religious masses rush to buy a book that offers aggressive retaliation against the sceptics. I do not know if it is correct to label Mr. Deepak Chopra as a religious person, but his point of view on miraculous violations of laws of nature is not in doubt. He is a very popular writer and lecturer. His very recent book Peace is the Way seeks to provide an antidote to the continuing scourge of war. He also takes the interesting point of view, as we have found in the Bible, that miracles do occur but come with a condition attached: you must have faith.

"Anyone can heal; the chief obstacle is that you believe that you can't." Deepak quotes this statement (p65) from a remarkable hands-on healer. And there is tacit agreement from Chopra. He goes on to quote an author that went from being a married lady and teacher to a divorcee and a job change in which she completed surrendered to whatever spirit wanted her to do. (p107) She studied the healing system that the Hawaiian Kahunas follow. The Kahunas emphasized "that our bodies are just mental projections and that we can heal them instantly using the mind." She then gives an example of a gash on her hand, blood oozing out. With limitless faith she "had the thought I can heal this." She looked down again and the gash was gone. Do we need to honour this with any kind of analysis?

Mr. Chopra does honour this event with this generalization: "The deepest mystery of all is that each person is more powerful than the seemingly iron laws that control us." (p107) Seemingly iron laws? When a soldier, criminal or terrorist holds a gun to our head, what would qualify for the description "seemingly?"

Chopra provides evidence that the focused consciousness of many peace dedicated people can change the destiny of the world. "If we can use the technology of prayer to bend a spoon with our minds, maybe we can also bend the whole world toward peace." (p65) Technology of prayer? Does Chopra know the meaning of technology? Bend a spoon!? He goes on the report how James Twyman, the most prominent person in the spoon bending movement, would go to troubled spots around the world to lead prayer vigils for peace. (p66) Of course there were instant violence reductions. At least by their statistics. Again: bend spoons!? Chopra states "the debunkers won't stop despite the fact that hundreds of people attest to bending spoons ... with their minds." (p67) Mr. Chopra, how many thousands were there to witness and attest to the much greater miracles of Joshua commanding the sun and the moon to stand still? With any scientific invigilation, the spoon will not bend. Mr. Chopra does not seem to be aware that if people could bend spoons with their minds, they would instantly turn this newly discovered capacity to a much more meaningful application. They would rush off to Las Vegas and put their money down. When the die comes to rest they would give it an instant little nudge to put it on the winning side. Next would come Roulette; have the ball jump from the undesirable number to the adjacent winning number! Should there be any believers in spoon bending, die rolling, or ball jumping, Las Vegas will welcome them all. Las Vegas will bet its money on the inviolability of the laws of nature and Las Vegas will be the winner. The spoon will not bend, the die won't nudge, the ball won't jump. The water won't change to wine, the wine won't change to blood. And we need not concern ourselves with a special cautionary wire to all pilots to warn them of sudden huge obstructions in the sky. We may rest assured: No mountain will rise up only to jump into the ocean!

# Chapter 4
# Atonement: Blood Preferred?

**Blood Preferred?**

"In atonement we come to the crucial point of the Christian faith." [Christian Theology, 2nd Ed. p781] Atonement, as the word clearly suggests, means to become one, to become unity with God. We will achieve atonement when our separation from God ceases to be, replaced, by oneness with God. If atonement has been achieved it will be the required balm that will force Satan, when he gathers his doomed victims, to pass over our souls. How is atonement to be achieved? Before addressing this momentous question we need to revisit the histories, beliefs and assumptions made by those who have previously attempted to answer that question.

We begin with God whiling away eternities in peace and tranquility. He is perfect: he is omnipotent, omniscient and benevolent, that is, all-powerful, all-knowing and good. Then he created the angels; we know not why. Quickly a large number of them left God to form a conspiracy of evil against God. These fallen angels organized themselves under the leadership of Satan. God's next creative impulse saw the earth, sun, moon, stars, animals and finally man, come into existence. No reasons for this creation are given. God places man, whom he has created in His own image, in the Garden of Eden. "And God saw everything that He had made and, behold, it was very good." [K.J.V. Amplified Holy Bible. Genesis 1:31] Instructions were given to Adam and Eve: two trees were pointed out, one the tree of life and the second the tree of knowledge of right and wrong. On the first tree, no further instructions were given; on the second tree they were told you shall not eat from it. Satan intervened. In serpent disguise, he persuaded Eve to eat the forbidden fruit, and she in turn, persuaded Adam to eat it also. Instantly they realized not that they had done wrong by disobeying God, but that they were standing there across from each other with fully exposed genitalia. How shameful, how wrong! The fall of man had occurred. They were evicted from the garden, never having taken the offered opportunity to eat from the tree of life, but with the knowledge of good and evil. Mankind proliferated. Their sinning knew no bounds. God's condition has changed dramatically. From a state of peace and tranquility he has descended to a state of frustration, fury, wrath and anger. He now has both the fallen angels and fallen man. His universe is shattered. How dare his recent creations refuse him what he desires with unquenchable intensity? Instead of a steady chorus of adulation and worship, together with consistent total obedience, these pesky critters are choosing to exercise their own free will, often choosing to violate God's laws. God's frustration quickly morphs into unbridled murderous anger. He reverses his previous assessment "and behold it was very good" into an amazing admission: "it repenteth me that I have made man." [K.J.V. Amplified Holy Bible. Genesis 6:6] It had been a mistake, an error, a futile, hastily conceived dream that had turned into a nightmare. What to do? He lashed out against his creatures in a totally futile murderous scheme: annihilate them all, excepting of course, Noah and family, some breeding stock and fish. It was to no avail. The sinning continued unabated. The main body of the Old Testament follows with Exodus, then the giving of the Mosaic Law to the Israelites. Then follows the annihilation of tribes inhabiting the promised land to make way for the new conquerors, the Israelites, under Joshua's leadership. God works with his chosen people. Even with powerful men of God delineating the right path, the Israelites waffle between obedience and iniquity, and consequently, between blessings and curses. The Old Testament gradually becomes a historical record of the up and down fortunes of the people writing the book, the Israelites.

When earlier attempts were made to answer the question "How is atonement achieved?" the previous summary of the Old Testament was accepted as given. No questions were raised concerning the internal logical consistency. No scientific scepticism was applied. We will indeed have to raise some questions. We have noted God's deteriorated state of affairs. From peace and tranquility He has descended into a morass where His preferred biblical descriptors are angry, wrathful, furious, regretful and even repentant. Only sporadically does God find respite from his prolonged state of fury. This happens when a penitent individual loads an altar with blood, fat, fur, etc., lights it and the acrid smoke rises providing a wonderful "soothing aroma" for God. In his unabated state of fury and anger, he redefines himself in a direction away from benevolence. Can God actually take pleasure in the punishment he will inflict on his creatures? "So the Lord will rejoice to bring ruin upon you, and to destroy you." [K.J.V. Amplified Holy Bible. Deuteronomy 28:63] Thus we have intolerable contradictions. Can a benevolent God take pleasure from inflicting pain? Can an all knowing benevolent God create angels, knowing that they will form a cancer of growing evil, metastasizing into every nook and cranny of God's subsequent creation, wherever Satan sees a potential foothold? When God created man did he know what he was doing? Is it possible for God to repent? How many times did God, all powerful, all-knowing and good, repent? Many times. Concordances list them all. Suffice it here to add that God anointed Saul as the first king of the Israelites. Subsequently, He realized that he had made a mistake: it repented God that he had anointed

Saul. [1 Samuel 15:10 and 1 Samuel 15:35] God then makes his choice for the next king known; it is David. And the inevitable wars follow when one king is replaced by another.

When God placed Adam and Eve in the Garden of Eden was it really his intention to have Adam and Eve running around in the buff in total ignorance and innocence? Would they find the tree of life and eat from it? Would they finally unlock the secrets of their genitalia and experience their first orgasm? Would Cain kill Abel without ever having any knowledge of right and wrong? Is it possible to kill Abel if he also ate from the tree of life and is thus immortal? In his book <u>How Good Do We Have to Be?</u> Harold Kushner states "Even as a child I was bothered by the biblical story of the Garden of Eden. A God who punished people so severely for breaking one arbitrary rule was not a God I wanted to believe in, especially since the story seemed to suggest that Adam and Even had no knowledge of what good and bad meant before they broke the rule." [p3] Kushner goes on to detail that it is the moral knowledge of good and evil that separates mankind from the animal world. Eating from the tree of knowledge was not sinful, it was a rite of passage from a simple animal existence to a more complicated moral human existence. Kushner then goes on to give an alternative ending to the story: <u>HOW THE STORY MIGHT HAVE ENDED</u>.

"So the woman saw that the tree was good to eat and a delight to the eye, and the serpent said to her, 'Eat of it, for when you eat of it, you will be as wise as God.' But the woman said, 'No, God has commanded us not to eat of it, and I will not disobey God.' And God called to the man and the woman and said to them, 'Because you have hearkened to My word and not disobeyed My command, I shall reward you greatly.' To the man, He said, 'You will never have to work again. Spend all your days in idle contentment with food growing all around you.' To the woman He said, 'You will bear children without pain and you will raise them without pain. They will need nothing from you. Children will not cry when their parents die, and parents will not cry when their children die.' To both of then He said, 'For the rest of your lives, you will have full bellies and contented smiles. You will never cry and you will never laugh. You will never long for something you don't have, and you will never receive something you always wanted.' And the man and the woman grew old together in the garden, eating daily from the Tree of Life and having many children. And the grass grew high around the Tree of the Knowledge of Good and Evil until it disappeared from view, for there was no one to tend it." [p32-33]

Now we will proceed to the New Testament. We will assume substantial familiarity with this portion of the Holy Scriptures. We know of the many signs and miracles, His call to repentance, his hatred of the sceptics; we know of his many parables, and his disciples. Finally, we know that his influence sufficiently incensed and threatened the existing power elite that a final reluctant decision was made to execute him. They utilized the standard Roman method of execution, crucifixion. Thus Christ died. With his disciples in a state of grieved bereavement, shock, disappointment and confusion, the account goes on to report that some people saw and talked to the resurrected Christ. His message did not die. But his disciples were left with the humiliating and nagging question: what purpose did Christ's death as a common criminal serve? They quickly rallied around the concept that Jesus had died "to offer his life as a ransom for many" [Matthew 20:28, Mark 10:45] Further, we know that the Greek word for ransom specifically means the payment of a price to free a slave or prisoner.

We are now ready to consider the main question "how is atonement to be achieved?" We will follow in the footsteps of influential thinkers and writers who have previously tackled this monumentally important question. We will attempt to understand how they reached conclusions that must sometimes, at least, remain utterly unpalatable to us. [The Biblical Doctrine of the Atonement. Lidgett, p1]. Many theologians have experienced "repulsion" from atonement accounts given by other theologians. We will begin with the uncontested champions of the Old Testament. How did the Israelites understand the atonement? How was it possible for them, in the past, now and in the future, to get right with God? The first aspect of the Jewish position was made clear in Exodus 32:32. Moses offers to substitute himself as an innocent sacrifice, for the sins of the Israelites. Spare them and let me bear their penalty. But the answer does not allow this vicarious atonement. "Who so ever has sinned" shall suffer for that sin. Jeremiah confirms it, "everyone shall die for his own iniquity." [Jeremiah 31:30] Yet again Ezekiel states "the soul that sinneth, it shall die" If A owes B money, C can very well come along and fully pay off A's obligation. B does not care who pays her the money. If A has separated himself from and also offended God by sinning and C comes along and offers to do penance to God on A's behalf, God will <u>not</u> accept it. In the Jewish conception then, there are no intermediaries on the sinner's behalf. Atonement happens when the sinner takes the required steps to make himself "right with God". What are these required steps? There is only one step. "all he need do to be forgiven is repent sincerely" [Judaism and Christianity. T. Weiss-Rosmarin, p54] This is confirmed by the Old Testament which we, of course, share with the Jews. "Let the wicked forsake his way, and the man of iniquity his thoughts; and let him return unto the Lord. And he will have compassion upon him, and to our god, for he will abundantly pardon." [Isaiah 55:7] Again in Ezekiel we read "but if the wicked turn from all his sins … and keep all my statutes and do that which is lawful and right, he shall surely live, he shall not die." And "cast away from you all your transgressions … and make you a new heart and a new spirit." [Ezekiel 18:21-30] What is required is repentance together with confirmation of sincerity by good deeds.

What does Jesus say? We have seen and documented earlier the Israelite heritage that Jesus knew so well. We were distressed to read "do not go to the Gentiles" where Christ confirms his position on the Israelites as the chosen people. When Jesus and also John, the Baptist, teach "Repent ye for the kingdom of god is near" we understand that repentance is the sole requirement to get right with god. Further, we read Jesus saying "Go and learn what the scriptures mean when they say instead of offering sacrifices to me, I want you to be merciful to others." [Matthew 9:13] It is again repeated in Matthew 12:7. Even the various sacrifices required under the Mosaic Law are no longer required, Jesus wants no sacrifices. He wants and sets the only requirement: you must repent and you shall validate your sincerity by doing good deeds, that is, by being merciful to others. He criticizes the Pharisees and the Teachers who seem more interested in obedience to the external appearance of the letter of the Law rather than a humble strict adherence to the spirit of the Law. Is there any indication from Christ that genuine repentance is insufficient to attain atonement? Is there any indication that a huge smog of guilt must first be lifted from all mankind before repentance will work? Is there any indication that without the substitutionary sacrifice of himself, even genuine repentance will do you no good? The Jews can see no such indication whatever. In Matthew 11:21 Jesus says "you people of Chorazin … and Bethsaida are in for trouble. If the miracles that took place in your towns had happened in Tyre and Sidon, the people there would have turned to God." We cannot expect a clearer statement. With the benefit of mighty signs and works, the people of Tyre and Sidon and even Sodom would have "repented in sack cloth and ashes" and would have turned to God. Is there any indication here of further requirements of vicarious atonement to set these people right with God? We have noted earlier, of course, the unfortunately unresolved question that arises from Christ's statement. Why not then supply the necessary signs and miracles? But for Christians there is a second even more debilitating question. Why did Christ have to die a horrible death when anyone can, perhaps helped by some signs, achieve atonement by making "a new heart and a new spirit?" It is of course this unresolved question that has made the

Jewish concept of atonement utterly unacceptable to modern Christians. Judaism cannot even begin to accept the rationale for a monstrous innocent sacrifice to atone for the sins of the guilty. But once the disciples had made and recorded the statement that Jesus had died "to offer his life as a ransom for many", there was no going back. Atonement by repentance alone was dismissed. The Jewish theory, while very attractive in many ways, leaves many problems unresolved. We will regretfully have to shelve their theory while we explore the Christian theories.

Now we will turn our attention to the Ransom Theory of Atonement. It is referred to also as the Classic View. It was the officially sanctioned theory of the Christian church from it's time of inception for over one thousand years. The Ransom Theory takes its beginning from Jesus' statement in both Matthew and Mark that he came to offer his life as a "ransom for many." Reading this statement, Origen of Nyssa reasoned that a ransom is a payment that is made to free a slave or a prisoner. The payment is made and the slave passes from being the property of him who accepts the ransom to him who paid the ransom. It is clear from Christ's statement who paid the ransom: Jesus did. Then came the critical question: to whom was the ransom paid? Clearly the ransom was paid by Christ on our behalf, but to whom? Origen believed that the parties at the table to negotiate this ransom transaction were the members of the Council of Heaven mentioned in the beginning of Job. Who were they? God, most certainly, and Satan, and God's son Jesus in his preincarnation state. Is it possible for the ransom to be paid by Jesus to his father God? Would this not mean that Jesus was purchasing our freedom from God; that we were to pass from the ownership of God to the ownership of Christ? Absolutely not! The only choice remaining open is that the ransom was paid to the devil, to Satan, and if the ransom was paid to Satan, ipso facto, Satan was proved to be the previous rightful owner of all people. And by Christ's ransom payment, we passed from being owned by the devil to being owned by God. These "facts" were deemed so incontrovertible, so rock solid, so directly taken from God's mind, that they became the substratum around which and toward which all events, logic and reason had to be dove tailed. If the devil had become the owner of all people, arguments had to be fashioned to show how, when and why he became the owner. And if Paul states that we have been bought for a "price" [1 Corinthians 6:20], Origen will develop the arguments to validate the transaction involving that "price" that Christ paid. In the cosmic struggle between the forces of good and evil, Satan established control and ownership over man. [Christian Theology. Erickson p792].

Satan established himself as world ruler with property rights over all mankind. Satan, the owner of all mankind? The sinless three great ancestors, Abraham, Isaac and Jacob? The great men of God including the prophets? The Old Testament heroes who did not have to die, but, instead, levitated directly up into God's presence? Was Origen aware of "the world and all that is in it belong to the Lord, the earth and all who live on it are His" [Psalm 24:1] Origen simply discarded any counter-evidence along the way and continued with his grand argument. The Council of Heaven met and God, fully recognizing Satan's ownership of man, enquires what kind of price Satan would be prepared to accept if God wished to purchase man back. Satan looks at Jesus and a "deal" is struck: give me Jesus' blood and you can have mankind back. God agrees. The partners to the deal "put their signatures" in place, meaning that even Satan could be fully trusted to honor his end of the deal. The crucifixion came off according to plan, Christ died, and mankind passed back to the ownership of God. What happened next caught the devil off-guard. Christ was resurrected on the third day and thereby escaped the clutches of the devil. Satan suddenly realized he had been "deceived"! [Christian Theology. Erickson p792] He had thought that even after Christ died that he would stay in his possession, but the deity of Christ had been hidden in Christ's human form. Never-the-less the devil adhered to the deal wherein he had been deceived: the ransom was paid. We became God's property. And Christ escaped from Satan's clutches.

What can we say for the logic in this theory of atonement? Are these the flights of fancy of mental midgets? But these theories held sway in the mighty Roman Catholic Church for over one thousand years. God's creation passed into the ownership of the devil? Scriptural passages ignored or brushed aside? God bartering a deal with the devil? God offering a deal too good to refuse? God assembling a very clever deceit? "The deity was hidden under the veil of our nature (he appeared human) so that as with ravenous fish, the hook of the deity might be gulped down along with the bait of flesh." [Christian Theology. Erickson p793] What a striking metaphor! The doltish devil having forgotten his interlude with Christ, testing him in the desert, signs onto the deal. Has he forgotten that three times he tested Jesus and Jesus, as God's son, spurned him every time? So our low I.Q. devil takes the bait! Theologians like Gregory and Rufinus loved the image of the fish hook and the bait. [Christian Theology. Erickson p794] In a very cleverly crafted deceit our wonderful God bests the leader of the forces of evil! Imagine the hook biting into the mouth of Satan! Can you see his scrunched up, ugly face with surprise, and pain writ large upon it? What a delicious morsel of 'schaden freude'! We will have no difficulty whatever discarding this theory of atonement. Indeed we find within it much reason for repulsion as did Lidgett in his book The Biblical Doctrine of the Atonement. But we continue to find it amazing and intensely dismaying that for over one thousand years, this theory was the official doctrine.

Next, the Socinian Theory of Atonement, or Atonement as an example. Socinus (16th century) felt that the "real value of the death of Jesus lies in the beautiful and perfect example which it supplies." [Christian Theology. Erickson, p783] We would immediately object to the use of the words 'beautiful' and 'perfect' in connection with his crucifixion. A pictorial or visual presentation of the grossest torture inflicted by man against man, is not beautiful. Had the Roman mode of execution been the much more humane later French mode, that is by guillotine, would that also have been termed beautiful or perfect? Socinus goes on. He agrees with Pelagius that 1) humans have the spiritual and moral fiber to do God's will; 2) that God does not require retributive justice and 3) that Jesus was merely human, he was not God incarnate. Thus Christ's death was in no way a substitutionary sacrifice. Then why did Christ have to die horribly? Socinus' theory is that he died to provide an example of Christ's love of God: "Jesus loved God so fully that he was willing to die, if need be, for the principles of the kingdom of God." [Christian Theology. Erickson, p784] What are the "principles of the kingdom of God" that required a horrible death of Christ? Here Socinus has evaded the essence of the atonement theory question. Can we accept Christ's death as serving no other purpose than providing an example of obedience? Other examples of obedience will not suffice? Can we accept that Christ is "merely human"? What do we do with the scriptural passages that indicate that 1) Christ was god incarnate, 2) Christ paid a ransom for us, 3) Christ himself bore our sins in his body on the cross … by his wounds you have been healed.

We are left in abject amazement that anyone would ever have attached any value to Socinus' theory of atonement.

Next the Moral Influence Theory of Atonement. Now, instead of the crucifixion demonstrating Jesus' love of God, it will be seen to demonstrate the love of God for Jesus. Peter Abelard who developed this theory, emphasized the "primacy of God's love, and insisted that Christ did not make some sort of sacrificial payment to the Father. Rather Jesus demonstrated to man the full extent of the love of God for him. It was man's fear and ignorance of God that needed to be rectified. This was accomplished by Christ's death." [Christian Theology. Erickson p785] Exactly how did the crucifixion affect man's fear of God? The Old Testament certainly attempted to instill the fear of God. Now God has changed His character, and now we need fear Him no longer? And the requirement by God that His son be tortured to death is to remove the fear of God? What was man to learn about God from the crucifixion? We have seen in the Old Testament God only required genuine repentance to set a sinner right with God. No sacrificial payment was required. Thus, even Peter Abelard evades the real question of the atonement: why did Christ have to die horribly?

In the event that man's fear of God and his ignorance of God was rectified to some degree, would that constitute a reason for proceeding with the worst of man's inhumanity perpetrated against the son of God? Is the end of abating the fear and ignorance of God somehow sufficient to justify the means, the crucifixion? Did God not have an unlimited number of pleasant means to attain the end of abating the fear and ignorance? This theory also fails.

Next the Governmental Theory of Atonement put forward by Grotius, 1583-1645, a lawyer. He states that God is like the ruler of a nation. He has the right to punish sin and must do so to maintain good government. Sin unpunished will have the citizens going wild. It is the ruler's prime responsibility to maintain law and order. But God's main attribute according to Grotius is love. In consequence God is inclined to clemency and gladly forgives many sins. But law and order must be maintained, thus, every so often, a demonstration of severity is called for. "God can forgive but He also takes into consideration the interests of His moral government." Grotius then sees "the horrible death of Christ as a deterrent to sin in that it impresses upon the sinner the gravity of sin." [Christian Theology. Erickson p788] Thus the shocking spectacle of Christ's crucifixion here serves the purpose of increasing the fear of God in his capacity to inflict pain. We remember in the previous theory we were instructed that Christ died to reduce the fear of God. Can both be right? If Grotius is right should we expect an improvement in the morality of man in consequence of Jesus' crucifixion? In the absence of such an improvement in moral government, are we to conclude that Christ's death was in vain? Grotius would have us believe that God is quite prepared to forgive all of our sins and would do so but will not because moral government would collapse. The threat of an eternity of hellfire in addition to the immediate effects of sinful behavior would be utterly inadequate to ensure moral behavior. The grotesqueness and cruelty of Christ's death could not leave any doubt in anyone's mind as to the capacity and inclination of the ruler to utilize the harshest imaginable punishments to maintain moral good government. We are very pleased to read that Grotius theory lacks a scriptural basis. They are the musings of a legal mind with an inherent bias in favour of heavy punishment for all, even minor infractions. He is obsessed with the fear of immediate anarchy if dramatic public punishment isn't forced upon the citizenry. The thought that the ruler and his government might themselves be the greatest instigator of immoral behavior has never occurred to him. Does Grotius' theory have a scriptural foundation? "We search in vain in Grotius for specific biblical texts setting forth his major points." [Christian Theology. Erickson p791] It will be with pleasure that we will reject the Governmental Theory of Atonement.

We have charted four theories of atonement: 1) Ransom 2) Example 3) Moral Influence and 4) Governmental and we have come away empty handed and distressed. We have seen holy scriptures studiously avoided and single passages elevated to trump status. We have seen contradictory images of God, merciful forgiver versus implacable punisher, and of Jesus, merely human versus God incarnate. We feel a sense of desperation as we approach the final and presently most accepted theory of atonement. It is called the Vicarious Satisfaction Theory of Atonement first set to paper by Anselm 1033-1109, Archbishop of Canterbury.

He wrote at a time when the feudal system held sway over most European peoples. There was no longer the universal presence of the Roman Law. The law you were subject to came directly from your feudal overlord. His whims and wishes were incontestable. And his status, his power, worth and prestige left his citizenry as tiny inconsequential specks. In Anselm's mind it was convenient and illustrative to view God as a feudal overlord. As such, there would be an expected tendency to punish very harshly. If, as a serf, you were caught stealing a carrot from another serf's garden, this inconsequential crime would be resolved by the famed eye for an eye, carrot for a carrot principle of justice. But if you, as a serf, were caught stealing a carrot from the feudal lord's garden, the inconsequential crime turns into a mortal sin. Your feudal lord would be expected to harbour a sensitivity to any crime that could unleash horrific punishment. Anselm then theorizes that God, like a feudal lord, possessed an infinite sensitivity for the sins of man. If you are the serf about to be horribly punished for the carrot theft, your extended family might come forward with money or property to offer to the feudal lord as a substitute for the punishment intended for the carrot thief. If the feudal lord is satisfied, the payment is made, the transaction is completed. That payment came to be called "satisfaction", and "vicarious" clearly means that the payment was made by someone else on behalf of the guilty party.

The Holy Roman Catholic Church was aware of many such transactions and finally experienced an "eureka" moment. Here was a wonderful means of topping up church coffers with money. Instead of the wonderful, simple "your sins are forgiven" statement, it would now come at a cost. The church would magnanimously accept payment from you for the forgiveness of your own sins and also the forgiveness of someone else's sins. With an insatiable appetite for more money, the church would remind you of the suffering of your deceased ancestors now in purgatory. A substantial payment to the "Lord" would release that soul from purgatory to the cool tranquil respite of heaven. At its peak (or perhaps lowest point) the church would accept payment from you for future sins. These payments were called indulgences. They were very common during the crusades. And even the holiest of the crusaders knew that the temptation to loot the riches and rape the women would be irresistible. So they purchased forgiveness in advance.

The inputs in Anselm's mind then came from common practice in his church and from the then most prevalent form of government. The infinite sensitivity of God placed a blanket of sin over all of man. This blanket of sin smog was so heavy and thick that man became utterly separated from God. Nothing man could do could lift this stain of sin, this heavy blanket. God had been infinitely offended by man and the balance sheet showed a mountain of debt owed by man to God. "Sin left unpunished would leave God's economy out of order." [Christian Theology. Erickson p797] In consequence, all of man was to be condemned, sentenced to hell forever. Thus we have an image of God creating man, watching them sin as He knew they would, then stoking the fires of hell in readiness for all of them. A loving god? A smog of sin covering all man? How can Anselm cast aside the "friends of God" and the chosen people of the Old Testament? But consigning all man to hell was too much even for Anselm. He finds an escape valve in the theories of Augustine. He quotes and adopts Augustine. God realized that He could not have all man go to hell because "some men must be saved to compensate God for loss of the fallen angels. Because fallen angels cannot be restored or saved, they must be replaced by an equal number of men. Thus God cannot inflict punishment on all humans. At least some of them must be saved." [Christian Theology. Erickson, p797] Again amazement and dismay! Again we see the unfettered imagination of incredibly arrogant minds quite prepared to probe into God's mind making their conclusions into God's conclusions. Questions: Is it O.K. to send all man to hell but it's not O.K. to send the fallen angels to hell? How much more are angels worth in God's economy than humans? Fallen angels cannot be redeemed? Is God omnipotent? For each fallen angel, God must, willy nilly, save exactly one human? Angels and men are now seen to balance in God's economy? If God made 10,000 angels of which 1000 fell, and He also made 30,000,000,000 people of whom all fell, He now finds himself in a tight spot. With great surprise, God now suddenly realizes that He must save 1000 of the 30 billion humans to set His economy in order? This reasoning is sufficiently repulsive and "off the wall" that the argument about the fallen angels has lately been purged.

Now, Anselm's updated theory of atonement, in simplified form, can be stated as follows:

1) Mankind sinned.

2) God in His total perfection and infinite sensitivity took infinite offense.

3) Nothing man could do could resolve or satisfy that infinite offense.

4) With the heavy sin smog blanket in place, God could not forgive any man's sin, even if that sinner comes forward with genuine repentance. In the Old Testament repentance may have been adequate. But now, to accommodate Christ's ransom payment, those Old Testament passages validating the repentance path have to be "deemphasized".

5) God's choices for man were limited to damnation for all man or a substitute of infinite dimension equal to satisfying His infinite offense.

6) God determined that this substitute of infinite dimension would be torture of the highest degree imaginable inflicted upon a god of infinite innocence and mercy.

7) God determined that this god of infinite innocence and mercy would be Himself incarnated in human form, posing as the son of God.

8) With the horrible death of Christ completed, the infinite offense of God was "satisfied".

9) With the infinite sacrifice completed, and "satisfaction" rendered to God, sinners could now get right with God by sincere repentance. Without Christ's sacrifice, repentance is useless. With His sacrifice, repentance would again, as in the Old Testament, achieve atonement.

The first thing that we would have to observe is that the end step (#9) of this theory of atonement brings us back to the clearly stated path to atonement given in the Old Testament. We are left with the question were steps number 1 through number 8 really necessary? Are they permissible?

How much of the Old Testament must be ignored, rewritten or purged to allow this theory credibility? Is it an act of integrity to scour the old Testament for prophesies that may point in the direction of a Messiah to come, while studiously avoiding all of those statements that leave no doubt whatever: God is always ready to accept a sinner back requiring only sincere repentance? Can we easily dismiss the intelligence and theological expertise of those who wrote the Old Testament and of the progeny of those writers who still practice the faith of their three great ancestors? The Old Testament is 100% clear. Genuine repentance will result in atonement. In modern evangelical language expressions such as "born again" or "accepting Jesus as your personal savior" or even "washed in the blood of the lamb" are preferred. But in practical terms they are the equivalent of genuine repentance: "a new heart and a new spirit." The modern expressions betray a compulsion to recognize Christ's horrible death as necessary. The heavy blanket of sin had to be lifted. But there is no evidence to be found in the Old Testament for this impenetrable blanket of sin. God did not impose that separation.

Suppose that God did put this mythical blanket in place. What does this do to His claimed characteristic of benevolence? When God determines how this blanket is to be lifted, He determines that the only solution satisfactory to himself involves the horrible death of His son. Or given the Trinity it becomes a suicide. What does this do to His claim of benevolence? One is tempted to consider the vast vista of alternatives available to omnipotent God. He could harden or also soften people's hearts. (Think of the Egyptians). He could intervene with power and glory. He could bring signs and miracles to bear that even the citizens of Tyre and Sidon would "turn to God". Let's unleash our own imagination on the process of Christ's horrible death.

When the Romans lay Jesus on the cross, and the first nail is held in place, and the hammer is raised, lightening bolts thunder down. A host of angels descends forming a glorious halo above and around Christ. A Charles Heston voice from heaven intones clearly "This is my son in whom I am greatly pleased." The scourgings of Christ heal. The blood disappears. The angel of the Lord commands the Roman soldiers to present the Roman leadership there immediately, and the Jewish rabble must assemble their Scribes, Teachers and Pharisees immediately. They arrive. And Christ bids the soldiers lay down their weapons before him. Swords, spears and battle axes rise slowly and then explode in a bright flash, only to settle back down on the people in the form of a gentle rain of mist. The Pharisees kneel and whisper humbly "there is no need for more signs". But Christ bids them all sit down. A child comes forward with a loaf of bread and another with a fish. The assembled multitude are about to share the most profoundly glorious meal imaginable. Christ states to them "be good to each other." God then intones "come home to me now, my son," and slowly Christ rises. He stops and again speaks "be tolerant of each other." And he ascends up and disappears surrounded by a halo of angels.

It was not to be. What a pity! And think of the plethora of much better options available to God omnipotent and omniscient. The important question is could God in his omnipotence have completed the atonement in any way other than sacrificing Christ? When theologians impute a mind fix onto God that implacably necessitates Christ's horrible death, God's nature takes on a hugely fear inspiring dark side. A loving God?

The Vicarious Satisfaction theory of Atonement must then be seen as having problems:

1) The Old Testament insists that God can be accessed; atonement can be achieved by genuine repentance.

2) The Old Testament does not allow an innocent party to take the punishment for the guilty party. No substitutions are allowed.

3) The Old Testament makes no mention of a blanket of sin severing all man from God.

4) The Old Testament prohibits human sacrifices; followers of Baal practice this abomination.

5) The central faith of Christianity that <u>God is love</u> is placed in question in view of

a) the blanket of sin cast over all of man by God's hypersensitivity to sin.

b) his choice of bloody torture as the active ingredient of atonement, it was the bloody torture that achieved "satisfaction"

c) A final state of affairs where most still fail God's tests and go to hell and few go to heaven.

d) God's dictate that once in hell, God will prevent the final silencing blessing of death; sinners will be kept alive forever to allow the torture to go on forever.

Why did Christ have to die a horrible death? The theories of atonement do not help us. The disciples, in their grief and confusion, sought to make sense of his death. They made ill-advised statements about paying a ransom. The result was the folly of the theology of ransom payments to the devil. Other efforts followed. Many shied away from shouldering God with an implacable demand for bloody torture. In the end, most theologians now do opt for the vicarious satisfaction theory. But it is in no way a satisfying theory. But at least it allows what the apostles said to be viewed as correct: "Christ died for us." It is as if the apostles in their unthinking haste to make sense of the situation made statements that were much later found impossible to understand, statements that were later found to be loaded with repulsive theological consequences. We know where the attempts to understand led the hugely distressed and sincere theologians. A quagmire, a theological nightmare. After a lifetime of effort, the results were found to be repulsive [see Lidgett] by the next generation of theologians. And so it continued. After many grueling attempts, we have no theologically acceptable answer to the question why Christ had to die horribly. That is, we have no theologically acceptable theory of atonement involving Christ's death.

A more secular point of view answers the question clearly and easily. Jesus became a focal point for many Jews of whom many hoped for a Messiah to free them of the detested colonial overlords, the Romans. The prophetess Anna "spoke about the child Jesus to everyone who hoped for Jerusalem to be set free (from the Romans)." [Luke 2:38] The angel Gabriel is sent by God to Mary, "The Lord God will make him king just as his ancestor David was. He will rule over the people of Israel forever." [Luke 1:32-33] The Romans were acutely aware that if the Jews rallied around a charismatic new leader, one with king David's military skill, the Romans would be defeated and ousted. Why did Christ die horribly? Because the Romans felt threatened. Haim Cohn's book, The Trial and Death of Jesus makes it abundantly clear. The Jews "did not kill Jesus" [p255], the Romans did. And Christ died horribly because once the Roman governor had passed the death sentence upon this threatening popular leader of the Jews, Jesus stood in line to experience death by the favored instrument of execution of the Romans, death by crucifixion. Did God order this horrible death? No, the Romans did. However, the Apostles made statements that made the secular interpretation impossible. Our theologians were then forced to try to make sense of God's plan of salvation. Jesus explained the plan to his disciples. Jesus said he would suffer, be tested, disapproved, rejected and put to death and after three days rise again. And "Peter took Jesus by the hand and led him aside and then facing him began to rebuke him. Then Jesus rebuked Peter, "Get thee behind me Satan because your mind wishes to please man instead of God." [Mark 8:32-33] Here we have Peter expressing his revulsion at Christ's plans. Please don't do it, Peter begged. And in his effort to stop the plan, Peter is likened to Satan. Does Satan then, like Peter, stand in opposition to Christ's plan? Of course! How can we expect Satan to be in support of God's plan for our salvation? He will do everything he can to thwart God's wonderful plan of salvation. Satan will do everything he can to prevent the crucifixion. And yet we read in John Chapter 13 that Satan conspired in favor of the crucifixion. Jesus' favorite disciple finally gets Jesus to point out the one of the twelve who would betray Jesus. He "dipped the bread and gave it to Judas, the son of Simon Iscariot. Right then Satan took control of Judas." [John 13:23-27] And Judas identified Jesus to those who came to arrest him. The gospel writer could not even get it straight in his own mind: does Satan support God's plan for salvation or does Satan not support the plan? Mel Gibson portrays Satan as gleefully rousing the Jews to ever greater blood lust. It seems that in the film, T*he Passion of the Christ*, Mr. Gibson was not prepared to contemplate Mark 8:32-33. The movie shows Satan fully in support of God's plan. It shows the blood thirsty rabble fully in support of God's plan. It never shows God in support of His own plan. God's plan became the epitome of the end justifying the means. It is not a satisfying scenario. Can it really be that when Satan and the rabble are at their rabid worst sinning, God could experience "satisfaction" at the scene? Could God actually think: 'I knew I could depend on them to see my plan fulfilled!?'

God was there. He saw the scourging. He saw the blood and the agony. And all the way through it He could feel His mountainous, infinite, load of pent up rage lifting. While in the Old Testament past He had experienced the "soothing aroma" of the acrid smoke of burnt offerings rising up to Him, now God experienced the soothing sights and sounds of the crucifixion. "My demand for punishment has been met, I have experienced "satisfaction" and the blanket of sin over all of humanity has been lifted." Or so our theologians would have us believe.

But be not deceived. The rage and wrath will continue. The pass rate at the Pearly Gates is still at best, miniscule. God's creation, man, is still not equal to His expectations. Our theologians would have God say: I know that as with Tyre and Sidon, just a few signs and miracles would have them turn to me. But I will not have it that way. Why make it easier for them? My requirements are heavy and will stay that way. Nearly all of mankind will, despite lifting the sin blanket, go to hell. And I will insist on a full measure of punishment. There, they will be burned to death with a special proviso: I will not allow them to die. Their agony and torture will go on forever. "I will have satisfaction" saith the Lord.

This theology of atonement together with our theology of eternal hell has turned the Christian God into a full scale psychopath. By the statement from the apostles "while we were yet sinners Christ died for us" they inadvertently turned God into a monster. Thus we have the evangelists preaching a God of love based on a theology of a psychopathic God.

It will be a powerful challenge to today's thinking theologians to devise a new theology of a loving, forgiving God, a new theology that sees Christ as a victim of the cruel Roman colonial authorities. Christ's death, seen as God's plan for atonement, must be consigned to that huge warehouse of misapprehensions along the way of progressing, thinking mankind. Perhaps we are ready to disempower those religious authorities who took advantage of the fear factor. A god that implacably insists on punishment panicked endless multitudes into abject subservience. Even now we hear "what would happen if you died tonight? Would your destination be heaven or hell?" And then the inevitable link is made between going to heaven and sending cash to the fear monger. The fear factor has worked very well for the religious authorities. But the Inquisition is no longer with us. Perhaps then there is hope that the theology of atonement by torture, and the theology of eternal hellish torture may also, mercifully pass and disappear into history. If the Ransom Theory of Atonement could hold sway as God's theory for over 1000 years and then be trashed, then it may also go the same way for the present Vicarious Satisfaction theory.The challenge that confronts the modern new theologian centers around the following biblical quotations:

1) The son of man came "to give His life as a ransom for many" [Matthew 20:28 and Mark 10:45] No ransom was required, no ransom was paid. His life was taken by the Romans.

2) "He himself bore our sins in His body on the cross" [Peter 2:24] Christ died on the cross for only one reason: the Romans killed him. Our atonement has to do with living by Christ's principles, not with the execution forced on him by the Romans.

3) "While we were yet sinners Christ died for us" [Romans 5:8] No. Christ died because the Romans killed him.

What would we gain by reevaluating the opinion of the apostles that Christ died for us? The immediate benefit is that the grievous slur against God, that our atonement theologians have imposed upon him, that He God, required the torture of His son to obtain "satisfaction" for the sins of man – that slur would be gone. The picture of God as a psychopathic monster would lift and disappear. A secondary benefit would be the reinstatement and validation of the many Old Testament quotations that have atonement with God available to all of us, then, now and in the future.

1) "What happiness for those whose guilt has been forgiven! … What

relief for those who have confessed their sins and God has cleared their record!" [Psalm 32:1]

2) "Let the wicked forsake his way and the man of iniquity his thought; and let him return unto the Lord. And he will have compassion upon him … and he will abundantly pardon." [Isaiah 55:7]

3) "But if the wicked turn from all his sins and keep all my statutes and do that which is right, he shall surely live, he shall not die … Cast away from you all your transgressions and make you a new heart and a new spirit." [Ezekiel 18:21-30]

4) "For out of thy great goodness, thou, O God, hast promised repentance and remission to those who sin against you, and in your boundless mercy thou hast appointed repentance for sinners as the way to salvation." [Prayer of Manasseh 1:7]

5) "Jehovah the Lord, a god compassionate, gracious, long suffering constant, true … forgiving iniquity rebellion and sin, and not sweeping the guilty clean away." [Exodus 34:6-7]

Can both be correct? Can it be true that Christ "offered his life as a ransom" payment for many and simultaneously maintain that it is true that God "appointed repentance" as the path to salvation? If the ransom statement leads to "repulsive" consequences should we not reconsider the Old Testament repentance path? Should God not prefer the path of repentance with a new heart and a new spirit over the path of blood and torture?

A final consideration, within this chapter, on atonement will be the reaction of Christ himself, if he were to be confronted with Anselm's Vicarious Atonement Theory, complete with its recent modifications. A thick sin smog covering all of humanity? Covering even the Old Testament friends of God, including the three great sinless ancestors, and all the prophets? Even the thought is blasphemous! God, the father, with a mountain of pent up rage, an implacable requirement for vengeance against man, a requirement now called "satisfaction"? That a spectacular torture orgy of an innocent god was required by God? That without this monster sacrifice, repentance fails? Jesus would have reminded us of his statement "Go and learn what the Scriptures mean when they say 'Instead of offering sacrifices to me, I want you to be merciful to others.' " [Matthew 9:13 and Matthew 12:7] He would have pointed out that the thinking of himself, the Son, and of God the Father, was, is and will be identical. Therefore no sacrifices. But be merciful. And the greatest affront to Christ of all: You are trying to tell me that the Scriptures, the Holy Scriptures, are wrong!? That repentance will not suffice when I have said so (repent, for the kingdom of heaven is near) myself and John the Baptist has also said the same? And you would deny the words of Moses, Jeremiah, Ezekiel, the Psalmist, Manasseh and Isaiah? You, the proponents of "Vicarious Satisfaction", are even worse than the Pharisees. Jesus would harry us out of his sight, just as he did the money changers in his father's house.

But the question as to why Jesus did have to die would be left, as before, unresolved.

# Chapter 5
# Free Will: The Powerful and Ruthless Preferred?

**The Powerful and Ruthless Preferred?**

The world abounds with suffering. Perhaps this has to do with news broadcasters who know that people will rush forward to see or read about disasters involving extreme suffering. Certainly the world also abounds with joy, even if joy is somehow less newsworthy. But joy would seem to be the natural outgrowth of a loving all powerful all knowing god. So it is the presence of suffering in this world that gives us cause for concern in the context of this book. So great is this dissonance - a loving god and a world full of suffering - that many Christian theologians have addressed this paradox. Their foremost motivation was, of course, a complete exoneration of god. They were possessed by a desperate zeal to maintain benevolence as a characteristic of god despite a world of his making, under his absolute dominion, a world full of suffering. A world replete with opportunities for miraculous interventions by god which would, with absolute certainty, reduce the suffering. If the theologians cannot exonerate god, the consequences, are momentously significant. A non benevolent god would be worse than a dead god. Would Christianity survive such a situation? Thus, many of the very best minds among Christian theologians have turned their full attention to this paradox: a loving god - a suffering world. These theologians have given many, and substantially different explanations in the multitude of books they wrote. They all, however, link the "free will" of man to suffering in the world. The blame is to be attached to man and not to God, they maintain. We will review the general problem of evil in the world in the context of the holy scriptures and the written record of theological thought. We will give special attention to the role of "free will" as it affects suffering in the world.

The Holy Scriptures leave no doubt as to the prime cause for suffering in this world. In addition to suffering in hell for our sins, both the yet to be damned and the yet to be saved, stand under God's unqualified commitment, that they will be punished here and now on earth. "But if you do not obey the Lord your God … then all of these maledictions shall come to you and light upon you." [New English Bible. Deuteronomy 28:15] What are all these maledictions? Three pages of the Bible are dedicated to them, from verse 15 to verse 68. Read all of them. It will suffice here to note these maledictions: 1) no one will be spared; 2) diseases: pestilence, wasting disease, fever, ague, eruptions, boils, tumors, scabs and itches "may these plague you until you perish" ; 3) the Lord put you to rout before your enemy. May your bodies become food for birds and wild beasts." 4) A woman will be pledged to you, another shall ravish her, 5) your sons and daughters will be given to another people, 6) you will eat your own children,

7) the pampered and delicate woman will eat her own afterbirth; 8) "'The Lord will bring upon you sickness and plague of every kind."

This can leave no doubt whatever in our minds. We have a demand for obedience from god, complete with a detailed listing of all the punishments that god holds in readiness for us should we sin. And as god was clearly aware, man would sin. Thus we can see that God's insistence on immediate heavy punishment is the prime cause for suffering.

But we are completely unprepared for what follows next: "Just as the Lord took delight in you, prospering and increasing you, so now it will be His delight to destroy and exterminate you" [New English Bible. Deuteronomy 28:63] OR "And as the Lord rejoiced over you to do you good and multiply you, so the Lord will rejoice to bring ruin upon you and to destroy you." [K.J.V. Amplified Holy Bible. Deuteronomy 28:63]

We are distressed beyond measure. We have a difficult time accepting God's insistence on heavy punishment. But we are much more than faced with difficulty that God will take delight in, or even rejoice, in imposing grievous suffering upon His creations. What kind of god can take pleasure in scourging mankind? In his book Suffering and God A.E. McGrath states "our suffering is His (God's) suffering" [p62] and even more clearly "God is deeply pained by our suffering" [p86]. This is the writer's considered opinion based on his conception of a loving god. Does McGrath know of Deuteronomy 28:63? Has this theologian dared to put pen to paper without the requisite study to form a learned opinion? Or has he, like many others, taken the liberty of expunging the more difficult portions of Holy Scriptures?

James Jones wrote the book Why Do People Suffer? The Scandal of Pain in God's World. His explanation for suffering comes in the form of a "clumsy analogy". [p17] You contract a disease that requires a medication that does cure the disease but has nasty, painful side effects. Of course you take the medication. In the same way God administers pain and suffering as the required medication to cause us to turn to God. Our bitter cancer medication prescribed to heal our disease is the best, and perhaps the only means to achieve the end, the healing of our disease. We are not all powerful or all knowing, and the medicine with the nasty side effects is for now, the best we can do. Is pain and suffering the best God can do to turn us to Him? He is all powerful and all knowing! Do we have to remind Him that it is His miracles that turn us most effectively and painlessly to Him? Don't impose pain and suffering. Remove the pain and suffering. And Jones, also, just like McGrath, is unaware of Deuteronomy 28. "He suffers when we suffer. His suffering is greater than we can imagine it … .[p42] Mr. Jones, please study the biblical text!

The biblical text speaks with implacable clarity. The words "take delight in" or "rejoice in" have clear meaning. We will not attempt to explain the biblical passages. But we will leave a big question mark over Mr. Jones and Mr. McGrath's books. We will leave the conclusion that God's implacable insistence on heavy punishment is the major cause of suffering in the world.

A second cause for the suffering we find in the world is a direct consequence of God's insistence upon testing His people. Does God test all people? Does He impose his suffering intense tests upon inveterate sinners and/or upon unbelieving Gentiles of whom God, in His wisdom, already has absolute certainty: they are among the damned? A test would reveal nothing new, nor would positive character development emerge from the test. The Old Testament suggests that especially one kind of person will be subject to God's tests. It will be members of His chosen people, and of those people, it will be His favorites. Among the tested we find Abraham, Isaac, Jacob and certainly Hezekiah, of whom the Holy Scriptures say "God withdrew from Hezekiah in order to test him and to see what was really in his heart." [2 Chron 32:31] An immediate problem arises. Is God not all knowing? Why does God not already know "what was really in his heart?" But these displays of not really being omniscient have occurred before. God has heard the "great outcry over Sodom and Gomorrah: their sin is very grave. I must go down and see whether their deeds warrant the outcry which has reached me. I am resolved to know the truth." [Genesis 18:20-22] It comes as a great surprise that God would need the information flow to Himself. There is no need to trust the truth of the outcry, there is no need to "go down and see," there is no need to make a resolution that will obtain the truth. It is embarrassing to have to remind God "but you are all knowing!"

Most of my career has been spent as a teacher and writer. In my teaching career, tests served the genuine purpose of ascertaining the level of proficiency of the students. I became, as most teachers, fairly adept at guessing a student's level of performance. But the tests remained necessary as I amassed considerable evidence that I was not all knowing. Some very important examination policies were in place in all institutions where I taught. Tests had to be fair. Tests were considered fair if three criteria were met: a) that tested had to conform with that taught, b) the level of the test had to conform to the level at which the material was taught, and c) that level had to conform to the level of capacity of the students such that the failure rate of the students would be somewhere in the vicinity of 15%. A failure rate of 50% would be to invite a visit from the dean. A failure rate of 75% and higher would invite a visit from the principal, letter of firing in hand. What will the failure rate be at St. Peter's desk at the Pearly Gates?

We see clearly that tests are everywhere among us in our educational situations and in our career and social lives. Now we are to contemplate tests applied to us by God. In his book The Purpose Driven Life by R. Warren, the statement is made that "Life is a test ... Words like trials, temptations, refining and testing occur more than 200 times in the Bible." [p42] Are God's test fair? "God keeps His promise and He will not allow you to be tested beyond your power to remain firm. At the time you are put to the test He will give you the strength to endure it." [1 Corinthians 10:13] The words "to endure it" contain a clear indication what the test might be like. Most probably it will involve intense suffering. The list of diseases that might form your test is endless: breast cancer, bone cancer, blindness, a broken hip, Hansen's disease, mental disorders, gout, etc. And the test may take the form of having the disease applied to a loved one who is in your care. The suffering can become unbearable. People's sanity, emotional stability and faith suffer extreme downturns. Can we consider such tests fair? In the aftermath of the Second World War, marked by no intervention from God, we have a general picture of a "continent that has abandoned its Christian heritage." [Father RaymondJ De Souza, National post, Ap. 18, 2005] Did the imposed tests exceed the power of most people to endure it? Of what value is the quotation, then, that the test will not exceed your power? If Mr. Warren were to see 10 people or 10,000 people from any of the many killing fields of the 20th century, whose faith in a loving God failed, what would he say? He would not see the forest for the trees! Or his spin doctors would maintain with ruthless judgment in their hearts you had the power to maintain faith in a loving God. You did not maintain that faith. You failed that test and it is entirely your fault. Prepare yourself for your consequences: "Eternity offers only two choices, heaven or hell." [R. Warren, p37]

We do not know whether the killing fields and death camps of the last century constitute punishment for disobedience, or some kind of monstrous test, or whether they are fully the consequence, the free will of man. [Which we will get to very soon] But the enormity of the crime and the enormity of the suffering is beyond all fathoming. Most of the books I have studied on the general topic of suffering in the world simply do not have the stomach to even try to reconcile a loving God, with the killing fields under His omnipotent charge. How shall a Jew, Protestant or a Catholic, be they dying of famine in the Ukraine, by poison gas at Auschwitz or by a bullet to the back of the head at Katyn, Poland, maintain faith in a benevolent God? They have seen the clearly established pattern. The scum of the earth, the bad guys in uncontestable power. Slave labour is your role. Your friends, with whom you fellowship as best possible, weaken and sicken and then are murdered. If I place myself in their situation, I would be forced to reevaluate God. Benevolent and all powerful? It cannot be. The prayers rising from the death camp victims are suddenly like the prayers of the 450 prophets of Baal imploring him to light the fire, to prove his existence. The death camp victims pray for an end to the arrogant, endless power of the Satanic overlords. The prayers to Baal went up: They invoked Baal by name from morning to noon, they cried louder, they gashed themselves. The death camp victims prayed silently, they invoked the name of Jesus, then they screamed to God Jehovah. And Elijah mocked the prophets of Baal saying "maybe your god is deep in thought, maybe he is on a journey, maybe he is asleep." Elijah recommended perhaps you should try calling louder! And the death camp guards mocked "keep praying, perhaps just a bit louder and I am sure your god will see to it that my gunpowder will change into mashed potatoes or even tapioca pudding!" We all know how Baal failed. And now, with total despair, we see the Lord God omnipotent fail just as Baal did earlier. And the immediate consequence of that failure let how many millions suffer and die?

Benevolent and all powerful? It cannot be! What are the options? Benevolent and impotent? It cannot be! Not benevolent but omnipotent? Or is he somehow not aware of the mess? C.S. Lewis has devoted much time and effort to this problem.

It seems impossible to arrive at any good answers. But it is certainly clear that if God imposes punishment on us for our disobedience, it hardly makes sense for us to expect a sudden change of heart on God's part where He would suddenly reach the insight that the punishment that He imposed was inappropriate. Do the crime, then do the time is an expression common among criminals. Provided that the punishment fits the crime, sinners will just have to "grin and bear" it. But the inequality of the distribution of such punishment by God would still be an utterly unresolved problem. People do the same sin. One gets punished horribly. The other goes unpunished.

It is note worthy here that these randomly applied punishments imposed by God, as we are to believe, are utterly identical to the common fate and fortune of mankind all around the globe. It appears to any scientific investigator that the link between violating God's law and the imposition of horrendous punishment is quite weak. It is not zero because a sinful life is a very irresponsible and dissolute life. If you live immorally and slothfully, you may fairly expect to experience more venereal diseases and famine. But when powerful foreign armies materialize you will be defeated, looted, raped, enslaved, murdered, etc. And your state of sinfulness or virtue will be utterly irrelevant. Likewise when a new virulent microbe assails your area you will succumb irrespective of your degree of faith or sinfulness.

If the suffering occurs due to God's intent to test you, can we expect a change of heart in God's mind where He suddenly has the insight that the test was somehow inappropriate? How shall we know if the suffering that God has imposed is punishment for previous sins or if it is a test that in no way implies a previous sin? Does God rejoice when He sees our suffering for previous sins and also rejoices when He sees the suffering resulting from yet another test that He has imposed? McGrath makes the extremely unhelpful statements that "God weeps alongside us" [p20] and the "pages of history are stained by the tears of God." [p20] And on page 85 he states that "suffering and death, like sin, are hateful to God." If they are hateful to God, it is certainly amazing how much of it may be found in the world.

It is claimed that suffering is a powerful character builder, that it results in greater spiritual maturity, that it draws us closer to God. We have questioned that point of view in the context of the death camps of the 20th century. Are there other means by which man may be built up in character, enhanced in spiritual maturity, and be drawn closer to God? We have the words of Jesus to answer that question: "Alas for you Chorazin, alas for you Bethsaida. If the miracles that were performed in you had been performed in Tyre and Sidon they would have repented long ago in sackcloth and ashes and their hearts would have been changed." {K.J.V. Amplified Holy Bible. Matthew 11:21] We have the failed application of miracles and mighty works in Bethsaida and Chorazin, but we are given absolute assurance from Jesus, they would have worked for Tyre and Sidon. Even Sodom, that den of iniquity, would still exist today if the miracles done in Capernaum had been performed in Sodom. The citizens of three cities could have experienced enhanced maturity, character strengthening and closeness to God at what expense to God and to those people? We have noted earlier that miracles cost God nothing in time and energy. Compare that to continual punishment for past sins on top of perpetual testing With what results? Do we have any scriptural basis that continual suffering will turn people en masse in the direction of repentance? Or does the sinning simply continue? For Tyre and Sidon we have a remarkable guarantee from Jesus himself. Miracles would have worked. The unsolved question is of course why this beautiful, painless and effective course of action was not followed.

We will at this time briefly compare the efficacy of suffering versus the efficacy of miracles and of signs in the effort to turn man to God. When John the Baptist sent his emissaries to Jesus with the question "Are you the one who is to come?", Jesus answered "Go and tell John what you hear and see: the blind will recover their sight, the lame walk, the lepers are made clean, the deaf hear, the dead are raised to life … " [Matthew 11:2-6] It is clear that Christ validates who He is by listing the miracles that He has performed. When Jesus left this earth his final instructions read "and these signs (miracles) shall follow them that believe: in my name they will cast out devils, they shall speak in tongues, they shall take up serpents and if they drink any deadly thing, it will not hurt them, they shall lay hands on the sick and they shall recover." [Mark 16:17-18] It is clear that the believers validate who they are by the miracles they perform. How effective were those miracles in turning man to God? "This deed at Cana – in – Galilee is the first of the signs by which Jesus revealed his glory and led his disciples to believe in him" [John 2:11] The miracle of turning water into wine had immediate and positive effect. "While many believed in his name because they could see the miracles he was working" [John 2:23] There can be no clearer statement that the miracles and signs were the key ingredient in turning man to Christ. Never is such a claim made for punishment and suffering. Very rarely do people move from non-belief to belief in consequence of suffering or testing imposed on them. How many Egyptians were turned to God by the suffering God imposed on them? But miracles? If ever there was an active ingredient that produced and strengthened belief, it was and is the signs and miracles. Jesus complained "will none of you ever believe without seeing signs and portents?" [John 4:48] Where would Christ's message have gone without the miracle of the resurrection? A large crowd of people followed who had seen the signs he performed in healing the sick." [John 16:2]

It is a wonderful thing to understand that the key to belief and faith is miracles and signs. There is no need for imposing horrendous punishments, there is no need to endure horrendous tests. Just extend that benign, warm, miraculous touch that ends the pain and suffering. And end the hegemony of the satanic overlords. It is a terrible thing to understand that this key to faith and belief, when requested of Jesus, often resulted in full blown rage and anger in Jesus. "It is a wicked and godless generation that asks for a sign." [Mark 8:12] "Why does this generation ask for a sign? I tell you this: no sign shall be given to this generation." [Mark 8:12] The key to faith and belief is fully and constantly available to Jesus but he is very reluctant to use it. Jesus gives us no idea why he harbours that reluctance. We have no reason to believe that performing miracles was difficult or demanding for Jesus.

But do we recall from Chapter 3 where the Bible report is quoted "He could not" perfom miracles in the presence of sceptics. It is very painful to seriously contemplate the situation where Christ can perform miracles (staged deceptions) with childlike or even childish, gullible believers around him; but surround him with intelligent "adult like" sceptics and he can not? But what is preferable? That he can but won't or that he won't and can't? Which situation is least painful? We know that Jesus was a man "singled out by God and made known to you through miracles, portents and signs." [Acts 2:22] Thus we have a conundrum: the key of miracles will be used selectively and rarely with powerful and benign effect. But punishment and suffering and testing will be universally applied with rare benign effect and frequent negative effect. I wish it were not so. How is it permissible for a benevolent god to refuse this constantly and readily available key to faith and belief?

Before we can leave the topic of suffering caused by testing, we must review the most prominent of all tests of people by God. The book of Job begins with a description of the man Job, a god fearing, righteous, and very wealthy man, blessed with a large family with seven sons and three daughters. "Now there was a day when the sons of god (Council of Heaven, N.E.B.) came to present themselves before the Lord, and Satan came also among them." How many sons does God have? And is Satan among them? Also present at this Court of Heaven is an "earthly scribe" who records verbatim all that transpires at that meeting. Thus we can read God's first question directed to Satan: "Where have you been?" It would seem an unnecessary question for an all knowing god. But Satan answers that he is just back from going "to and fro in the earth and walking up and down in it." We note that only God and Satan actually participate in this meeting: all others remain silent. God continues "have you noticed my servant Job … a blameless and upright man?" Satan responds that Job is god fearing and righteous only because God has protected and blessed Job in every way. Satan then challenges God to test Job: "But stretch out your hand and touch all that he has and then he will curse you to your face." Again, God appears to be less than all knowing. God already knows if Job would pass or fail the test. The test is thus unnecessary. With a total lack of compassion, God accepts Satan's challenge and authorizes Satan to proceed. "All that Job has is in your hands." The test is ruthless beyond comprehension. His vast wealth is stolen by others. His seven sons and three daughters die in a whirlwind directed by Satan. Job is the one to be tested but the "collateral damage" includes all of his children and most of his slaves. The Court of Heaven is reconvened and again our scribe reports on all proceedings. God starts with the same question "where have you been?" He adds that Job has passed the test. "You (Satan) incited me to ruin him without cause but his integrity is still unshaken." Did God not know this in advance of the test? Was the test necessary? Does the death of his children and the slaves matter at all? Can an all powerful, all knowing, and benevolent God allow himself to be incited by anyone, especially Satan, to ruin Job without a cause? It gets worse. Satan now issues a second challenge: "Stretch out your hand and touch his bone and his flesh and see if he will not curse you to your face." [Job 2:4] Again God allows himself to be incited by Satan. In a second display of a complete lack of compassion, God authorizes Satan to proceed with the test: "So be it, he is in your hands, but spare his life." We note that God nowhere suggests the purpose of the test is a strengthening of Job's (or anyone else's) faith. The test proceeds to answer Satan's challenge and to address God's lack of omniscience. Satan goes to work immediately afflicting Job with running sores from head to foot. Thus, the first portion of the book of Job ends.

The second portion of the book of Job proceeds on the basis that the first portion does not exist. In the midst of Job's suffering, his three very erudite friends arrive to offer comfort and advice to Job. Job, knowing nothing about the Council of Heaven and the compassionless dialogue between God and Satan, raises the question "why is this happening to me?" He curses the day he was born. "Why should the sufferer be born to see the light? Why is life given to men who find it so bitter? They wait for death but it does not come, they seek it more eagerly than hidden treasure." [Job 3:20-21] The question is critical because Job is fully and correctly convinced that he has done no wrong. Then why this horrendous suffering? His three friends launch PhD dissertations to answer Job. Since God is just and would never punish without cause, it must be that Job has indeed sinned grievously. All three, Eliphaz of Teman, Bildad of Shuah and Zophar of Naanah try to persuade Job of having sinned. To no avail. Job continued to insist on his total innocence. Finally, a fourth PhD candidate arrives. Elihu, son of Barakel, repeats what the other three have said before: "Far be it from God to do evil or the almighty to play false! For He pays a man according to his work and sees that he gets what his conduct deserves. The truth is, God does no wrong, and the almighty does not pervert justice."

[Job 34:10-12] But Job continues to maintain his innocence. We are left with the quandary: are the four learned gentlemen right who maintain that since God is just, Job must have sinned to deserve his suffering or is Job right? We understand that if Job is right, God has been unjust in causing Job to suffer without cause. It is note worthy here that none of the five parties to this second portion of the Book of Job have even remotely contemplated the possibility that Job, despite being totally faultless, is being tested. The concept that a faultless man might be tested in such a horrendous manner was not in the realm of the possible for any of them.

The third part of the Book of Job provides a response to Job directly from God. We are to believe that "the Lord answered Job out of the tempest." But the god that answers out of the tempest is not the same god that we met in conversation with Satan in the first portion. The writer of this portion is utterly unaware of the first portion. There is no mention of God's authorizations to Satan to test Job. God's answer starts as follows: "Who is this whose ignorant words cloud my design in darkness? Brace yourself and stand up like a man; and I will ask questions and you shall answer." [Job 38:2-3] This god will in no way answer Job's question "Why is this happening to me?" There will be no admission of the compassionless dialogue between God and the devil. Here the "answer" is not an answer at all. As with Esdras's questions, the response comes with arrogant anger. Esdras is asked to "weigh me a pound of fire or a bushel of wind or bring back a day that has passed." Job is asked by this god

a) were you there when the earth was made, when it's dimensions were settled?

b) have you visited the storehouse of snow or the arsenal for hail?

c) did you give the horse it's strength?

d) do you have an arm like God's?

e) have you considered the crocodile, the chief of beasts which has firebrands shooting from his mouth, sparks coming out with breath that sets coal ablaze? [Job 41:19-21]

Fully dazed and cowed by all these impossible questions, Job realizes that the message here is a simple one; he was not allowed to ask the question, "Why am I made to suffer?" It is difficult to understand why this question was not to be asked of God because he already did answer it in the first portion of the Book of Job. Again, this portion of Job was unaware of the first portion of Job. Secondly, the fire breathing crocodile is total nonsense. God knew then as he knows now that crocodiles do not breath fire. But the writer of Job was not so well informed. It raises the question did God really speak out of a tempest? Or did the writer feel that his answer to Job's question would gain in status and panache if he claimed that his answer was really God's answer?

There is a short epilogue or a final fourth portion to the story. After having repented, of raising the question "why am I suffering if I am innocent?", Job is asked to intercede on behalf of Job's friends because they did not speak of God as they should have. The Lord then restored Job's fortunes and doubled all his possessions. He had seven more sons and also three more daughters. As a top-up for his compensation Job was blessed by having those three daughters, Jemimah, Keziah and Keren Happuch declared to be the most beautiful women in the world. Thus "Job's daughters" has come to mean gorgeous, ravishing women.

In summary what can we learn from Job? It is a first biblical attempt to explain why bad things happen to good people. Harold Kushner's book, by that title, addresses the question in a modern way. The Book of Job starts with a full answer to the question, then proceeds to a very academic and very different answer, and finally we have God taking the position that Job's question was impertinent and inappropriate. The academic answer is still very much respected among those of Jewish faith. God, being just, simply would not and could not test Job brutally with complete disregard for Job and all the collateral damage. Job, therefore, had to have sinned. The same logic was applied when the Jews suffered horribly in the Holocaust. Many Jewish theologians took the point of view that since the punishment was vastly horrific, the sin of the Jewish people must likewise have been vastly horrific to justify the punishment. Other Jewish theologians felt that there could be no sin among the Jews that could ever justify the Holocaust as punishment. Many Jews lost faith in a benevolent god.

The image in Job of a compassionless god authorizing Satan to go forward with the tests is very disturbing. The dissonance from one portion of the book to the next is also disturbing. And we are left with the argument of Job's friends "the almighty does not pervert justice." Then we are told that Job was innocent and did not deserve the suffering. We are distressed by the conclusion that Job's friends then had to reach: the almighty does pervert justice?

A third important cause of suffering in the world is the impact of the free will of man. The free will of man is a very complicated philosophical topic. Many books and treatises are available to unravel or even obscure what is meant by "free". However, all of us have a fairly clear concept of what free will means and how it impacts on our lives. And we have an equally clear concept of what it means to be deprived of ones free will. The watchword of many western democracies is the word freedom. In the hands of business people and politicians that word, freedom, will experience untold convolutions. But despite these efforts to bend, twist and obscure the meaning, a core understanding remains. It is that core that we will deal with here.

We will immediately note that a completely free will does not exist. So many things in our lives are subject to iron clad laws: we must eat, we must breath, our physical bodies have non-negotiable rules attached at all points. As I have indicated to many students, the most important choice in your life is the choice of your parents. They realize the implication immediately. In the determination of the DNA material that will architecturally constitute you and in the determination of who will care for you, you have no say whatever. In the choice of what religion you will adhere to, the impression of free will quickly yields in view of the fact that 98% of all Muslims are born of Muslim parents, 98% of all Catholics are born of Catholic parents, 98% of all Jews are born of Jewish parents. A small degree of personal choice does seem to be there. Criminals convicted of crimes of violence tend to be regarded by everyone as free agents. They chose to do the evil act and we tend to have an easy time prescribing the well deserved punishment. But our scientists, operating at the cutting edge of physiology and psychology, have discovered a difference in the physiology of the brain between these violent criminals and the average well behaved citizen. The brains of these criminals respond differently to the minor and major irritations that we all have to face. That portion of the brain that allows us to "chill out" when angered does not work as well in these criminals. If I had the choice of a brain with excellent anger control characteristics versus a brain that tends to escalate a provocation into blind anger, I would have an easy choice to make. But the choice is not ours. We recognize that on deeper analysis, our free will tends to be diminished.

We remain convinced that we have the freedom to choose to go to school, to say no or yes to drugs, to choose abstinence in sexual matters, to rob a bank, to donate to our church, to become a terrorist or to become a priest. At least given the circumstances of a citizen in a western prosperous democracy, our freedom to choose is largely unfettered. This, of course, changes dramatically when the government for the people and by the people becomes a dictatorship. The leader and his clique plus a number of sorely deceived citizens take control and those in opposition are silenced. When those who initially supported the dictator realize what a monster they have helped to put in power, it is too late. They too will be silenced. When evil people have the propaganda, economic, police and military might of a government, we have a guarantee for untold suffering. People's freedom will be gone. Or if you prefer, you have the choice of doing what is right, stating loudly and clearly the crimes of the power elite, or be silent on the crimes of the government and in consequence you and your family will live. I would not consider such a choice to be free. Life, in particular if you have a family, must come first. I hope I will never be put in a position to make such a choice.

Evil governments. Thugs and sadists raised to the status of all powerful government officials. With the all powerful weaponry that only governments can assemble. How shall we deal with them? The bible is unspeakably dismaying in this regard: "Obey the rulers who have authority over you. Only God can give authority to anyone and he puts these rulers in their places of power. People who oppose the authorities are opposing what God has done, and they will be punished. Rulers are a threat to evil people, not to good people. There is no need to be afraid of the authorities. Just do right and they will praise you for it. After all, they are God's servants." [Romans 13:1-4] God's servants!? Only God can give authority to anyone? Stalin, Hitler, Pol Pot, etc.! God put these monsters in their places of power? The very best we can do is assume that the writer's grasp of history and political science was so limited that he might, in retrospect, have wished he could retract his words. Certainly his words were used to great advantage by kings and dictators. We know how difficult it was to remove those "divine right" kings. We also know of dictators quoting these scriptural passages to validate their all powerful status.

Can we hope for God's intervention when the thugs and sadists have power firmly in their grip? We know the untold suffering that follows in the wake of evil governments. Our expectation then is that God would intervene to curb the criminal activity of such an evil government. But we have countless examples in the immediately passed 20th century of evil governments continuing with their horrific deeds with no intervention from God. Many have to be brought down by military might where "good" nations ally themselves with "bad" nations to defeat a "bad" nation only to empower our allied "bad" nation to super power status. How many people suffered and how many people were murdered in the Soviet gulags? With precious little evidence of God's intervention we are again left in a quandary: If God can intervene but chooses not to intervene can we continue to view God as benevolent?

In the case of Job, we saw a servant of God, a righteous man subjected to unfathomable suffering. Do we now, with thugs and sadists in power, see

God choosing to <u>not</u> send some extensive suffering to these criminal monsters? Do we not have a promise from the Old Testament that God will rejoice and take delight in destroying and exterminating those who do not obey the Lord? Do we now have an exemption from punishment for the most evil of all people? We might be forgiven for also taking delight in seeing these evil people punished by God, if only He would do so. The pitiable good man Job "takes it in the neck" and the truly most monstrous of all men are to be exempted? Can it be so?

Our thoughts fly back to Job and momentarily our imagination takes flight. A third Court of Heaven is convened and again the "sons of God" are present. Again God and Satan are the only active participants. God starts. "Where have you been?" Satan: "I have been ranging over the earth from end to end." But be continues: "Have you considered my servants? They are Satan worshipers and are evil to the core: they are dominated by pride, covetousness, lust, envy, gluttony, anger and sloth with a full measure of arrogance and sadism thrown in." God responds, "Do not your servants have good reason to be Satan worshippers? You have surrounded them with luxury and pleasure. Stretch out your hand against them, test them by intense suffering and see if they will not curse you to your face!" Satan: What!? Me, test my servants with suffering to see if they will curse me? Absolutely not! I don't do that! Furthermore, isn't this what <u>you</u> are supposed to do? Did you or did you not state clearly in Deuteronomy 28:15 "But if you do not obey the Lord your God by diligently observing <u>all</u> His commandments and statutes which I lay down upon you this day, then all these maledictions shall come to you and light upon you?" And God remained silent.

Back to reality. God did not intervene in the horrors of our history. The suffering was endless. God could have intervened and should have intervened but chose not to. Do we have a benevolent god? Do we have a god that is prepared to act on his promise in Deuteronomy, chapter 28, to punish those who most flagrantly defy his commandments?

Mr. C. S. Lewis felt himself equal to the challenge of unraveling the question of God's lack of miraculous intervention in our world when thugs and sadists take control of our lives. With the desperate motivation to avoid the conclusion that God cannot be benevolent if He refuses to intervene, C. S. Lewis launches into his book <u>The Problem of Pain</u>. He begins with a statement from Thomas Aquinas: "Nothing which implies contradiction falls under the omnipotence of God." Here we have a reasonable clear statement that God cannot make a rock that is both hard and soft. An object, even in God's omnipotence, cannot be made to be at a distance of ten miles and simultaneously 10 inches from another object. We can agree that if something is self contradictory, it is absolutely impossible. Then comes a quantum leap. "If you choose to say 'God can give a creature free will and at the same time withhold free will from it' you have not succeeded in saying anything about God: meaningless combinations of words do not suddenly acquire meaning simply because we prefix to them the two other words 'God can' " [p16] But Mr. Lewis does draw the conclusion from that statement that either God confers free will upon man or He does not. It has become a simple black and white issue and any adjustments of the two results in contradictions. It will be either scorching hot or bitterly cold. Has Mr. Lewis heard of thermostats? And even God cannot do the intrinsically impossible. Mr. Lewis has peered deeply into God's mind and has returned with a conclusion that now becomes God's own conclusion. Mental intercourse with God. What dangerous territory! We think of the Ransom Theory of Atonement which held sway as God's answer to the question of atonement for over a thousand years. And then someone determined that it was grossly erroneous; that intellectual intercourse with God turned out to be a man's intellectual intercourse with himself. We think of the crusades, the indulgences, the inquisition. At some point some man or men took the justification for these actions directly from the mind of God, or so they were convinced. Later, we became convinced that these justifications did not at all issue from the mind of God. There were man's fabrications.

Free will or no free will as a black or white issue!? We know every country in the world has a police force. These people have been charged with the responsibility of limiting the exercise of free will. You are simply not allowed to do anything you want. If you cross certain usually common sense boundaries you will find yourself arrested and deprived of freedom. The necessity of limiting or curbing the free will of people is recognized everywhere. Indeed, an effective police force is universally recognized as an essential ingredient in what we call freedom. In educational institutions we limit and curb the free will. As parents we lay out behavior parameters that effectively limit the free will of our kids. You may pinch lightly, you may shoot with a water pistol but you may not do an activity that involves a high risk of hurting yourself or others. We have severe curtailments of our free will with respect to the life and property of others. This is so commonplace and so natural that it becomes cause for serious misgivings that Mr. Lewis cannot conceive of the possibility of a limited free will. Instead of a black and white proposition, it is a thoroughly gray issue. Just a few of the many options that even my flawed brain can assemble include:

1) every person shall have free will only over himself - thus God will see to it that you cannot curtail others free will, or hurt them;

2) every person shall have free will over herself and will be allowed to hurt others only "slightly";

3) everyone shall have free will over himself but shall have a maximum free will to do to others everything except "murder";

4) everyone shall have complete free will with the rigidly enforced proviso that after three "major" sins, you're out, as in three strikes and you are out;

5) everyone shall have complete free will but cannot exceed murdering more than 10,000 people, etc.

Clearly it is possible for God to endow us with a partial or limited free will. But this does not fit at all with Mr. Lewis' argument. He proceeds on the basis that it remains a black and white issue.

"People often talk as if nothing were easier than for two naked minds to meet or become aware of each other. But I see no possibility for doing so except in a common medium which forms their environment." [p18] What childish revelations. Have you ever been in a situation where that common medium was not present? We live in that everpresent necessary common medium. But Lewis goes on. For us to effectively communicate with one another that common medium must be consistent. It cannot change from one moment to the next. If only one individual existed it would be conceivable to have that external environment so constituted to, at all times, maximize the pleasure of that one person. But if more than one individual exists, all with their free will, the external environment, to allow communication, and to be fair to everyone, must be the same for everyone. Therefore, we have the inexorable laws of nature. Therefore, when humans engage in warfare, Napoleon turns out to have been right: the army with the biggest and most guns will win. Lewis concludes his argument with, "So it is with the life of souls in the world: fixed laws, consequences unfolding by causal necessity, the whole natural order, are at once the limits within which their common life is confined and also the sole condition under which any such life is possible. Try to exclude the possibility of suffering which the order of nature and the existence of free will involve and you find you have excluded life itself." [p22] His conclusion is clear. There are inexorable laws of nature. And God endowed us with a limitless free will. Therefore, we will suffer and it will be our own fault. God does not and will not intervene because he cannot. If he did, it would be self-contradictory and therefore absolutely impossible. Case closed. And God remains benevolent.

It is embarrassing to study the transparently flawed argument presented by Lewis. And it is humiliating to recognize that Christian theology draws a great deal of comfort and assurance from it. Perhaps it is his conclusion, which exonerates God from the charge of nonintervention, that is so enticingly attractive that people choose not to analyze the argument in any detail. However, Mr. Lewis himself must have experienced an "anti eureka" moment looking at his completed argument. Was he suddenly aware that he had painted himself into a corner? Or did he realize, with bumps and bruises all over his body, that he had just cut off the branch he was sitting on? What happens to the foundation book of Christianity, the Bible, if miraculous interventions by God are not possible? Any intervention would "exclude life itself." Was not the origin of the world, the entire universe one huge miraculous act of creation? How many miraculous interventions by God happened in Exodus? "In full view of all you people, I will do such miracles as have never been performed in all the world or in any nation. All the surrounding people shall see the work of the Lord." [Exodus 34:10] Do you remember the parting of the waters and the drowning of the evil Pharaoh? And the New Testament. How many miraculous healings? How many raised back to life? Inexorable laws of nature!? Can you imagine Christ being confronted by Lewis: You cannot do all these signs and miracles because it would be self contradictory and therefore absolutely impossible! I can imagine Christ's response: "You are exactly the person I had in mind when I said 'My father, Lord of heaven and earth, I am grateful that you have hidden all this from wise and educated people and showed it to ordinary people. Yes, Father that is what pleased you.'" [Luke 10:21]

What to do? Mr. Lewis despaired of tackling the problem anew. To start over again was out of the question. So without any changes whatever to the entire argument Mr. Lewis now finds that a small number of violations of the laws of nature, that is miracles, is not self contradictory and therefore absolutely impossible. It is only when you have a "large" number of miracles that somehow suddenly the absolutely impossible is encountered and "life itself" would be excluded. And then he proceeds to tell us what that small number is: add up all the miracles that happened in the Bible and then you have the total, that small number of miracles is the number that is permissible. Life remains possible. However, the next miraculous intervention would be the first one to involve the absolutely impossible. And we are to believe, according to Lewis, that then life itself would be excluded. How can 10,000 miraculous interventions be totally okay but the next one, the 10,001 miracle, is so categorically different that life itself would be excluded? The final conclusion from Lewis is that miracles must be "extremely rare" (p22)

In the final effort to bolster his argument Lewis makes the statement "in a game of chess you can make certain arbitrary concessions to your opponent which stand to the ordinary rules of the game as miracles stand to the laws of nature" [p22] Does he dare to compare a move in a chess game to healing a leper? Does Lewis know the game of chess? Does he know that a concessionary move is made for one of two possible reasons, a) to level the playing field when an expert (grand master) takes on a beginner? OR b) the move has the immediate appearance of having lost a significant player but creates new strategy opportunities that become only too evident later. How can the beautiful miracle of Jairus' dead daughter brought back to life be compared to a chess move? With whom was the playing field leveled? Or was it a devious plot with the loss of a significant player?

This then was the effort by Mr. Lewis to exonerate God. And his effort has been viewed by many as "perhaps the most articulate explanation" [Where is God When It Hurts. Philip Yancy, p15] for the non intervention of God in the suffering of mankind. Perhaps it is an exoneration for Lewis to note that when he was assailed more personally by the savagely painful disease of bone cancer in his wife, his own arguments about God's non intervention faded more and more in significance and coherence. However, recanting on his argument only serves to revive the question that gave rise to the argument. That original question, we remind ourselves, is "If God can intervene to alleviate suffering, why does He choose not to intervene?" If we cannot answer that question, God's benevolence is precariously on the line.

God endowed us with free will, every one of us. He must have had god reason to endow us with this unlimited power of choice because it came at a huge cost. It certainly empowered the thugs and sadists to proceed with their activities. My own relatives have reported from a variety of bible schools that God's reason for endowing us with a free will was because "God does not like robots." We don't want to be robots, but we want limitations on free will to prevent some of us from becoming powerful and arrogant robots of evil. Thus, in a micro-cosm, we have an "evil" person attacking and abducting a "good" person. The evil person, almost invariably, is the armed and ruthless one. The evil person makes short shrift of the free will of the better person and the free play of the sadism of the evil person ensues. Suffering happens. Unrestrained free will for the powerful and ruthless. And what of the free will of the "good" person? With mouth gagged, hands and feet shackled, bleeding and hurting, what free will is left? Given the choice of supporting the free will entitlement of the good person versus the free will entitlement of the evil person, what will God do? All that the victim can do is mumble a desperate prayer for intervention by God. Again, the image of the desperate prayers of the 450 prophets of Baal come to mind. Baal did not hear. Baal did not respond. Multiply this scenario by several millions and you will see the killing fields, the gulags and the concentration camps of the last century. Did our god hear? Did he act?

A fourth major cause of suffering in the world derives from God's unwillingness to inform us what his position is on many different issues. In his book Suffering and God, McGrath states "God has already taken the trouble to tell us exactly what He is like." We will disagree whole heartedly with McGrath. Let us begin in the Old Testament. "You shall not allow a witch to live." [Exodus 22:18] With the logic of C. S. Lewis we will argue that the rule clearly implies that there is such a person as a witch. If God has let it be known that witches do in fact exist and further requires that we stone, burn or hang all witches, one critical requirement in the instructions has been left out. How shall we identify them? Do we know God well enough to somehow figure out how to discern a genuine witch from a hapless, innocent old woman, or even a hapless innocent beautiful young girl? There were not wanting sincere Christian thinkers who probed into God's mind, or so they thought, who devised the tests to determine the identity. The Pope of the Holy Roman Catholic Church issued the Papal Bull Hammer Against Witches and the hunts for them and the executions of them went forward. The tests for identity were childishly foolish or fiendishly callous or both.. A scale was constructed with a bible set on one side. The accused was commanded to step onto the other side. If the accused weighed more than the bible, the church officials had solid evidence directly from God that they had caught a witch.

How many of the church officials were God fearing righteous men? While we can be sure that not all of them were, we can be totally certain that some were. What answers did they get from God when prayerfully they raised the question: should we really kill them? Is the test reliable? They went back to the rule "you shall not allow a witch to live" and appeared to get the answer "it may be an ugly business but it must be done and most certainly God would intervene in the scale test if the accused was innocent." They reminded themselves that they were men of faith, and that they had the full faith that God would guarantee the correct outcome in their identification process. To test that process would be both to test God – not permissible – and to betray an inadequate faith level. Other tests were devised. Christian theology, at that time, held that the devil could at any time make a physical appearance on the earth and impregnate a woman. And where the devil touched the woman, he would leave behind tell tale markings. Therefore, the church officials had reason to eagerly gather around when the accused party was commanded to undress, bend over, spread buttocks and labia, to be gawked at and probed by the officials. "One of the favorite ways of determining the guilt of a witch was through a trial by water, in which they took the accused to the river, tied her hands and feet together so that she was bent over in a squat, and then threw her in the water. This was an old Babylonian idea, noted in the Code of Hammurabi. The idea was that the holy river would decide a person's fate, drowning the guilty and floating the innocent. Thus justice was something even the waters of the river would attest to. However, the Assyrians turned this on its head. According to their rules, if those thrown in floated, then the waters rejected them, and they were guilty of witchcraft. If they sank, then the waters received them, and they were innocent. We are aware that the normal physiology of a woman gives her a higher ratio of adipose tissue than that ratio for a man. Thus the Assyrian method of witch identification contains an inherent bias against women: they will tend to float, males tend to sink: females will be found to be guilty, men will be found innocent. The Assyrians had an odd sense of humor. Of course, the onlookers had to be quick, or the innocents would drown before they could celebrate their acquittal. This Assyrian tradition was the one that traveled into Europe long before Christianity appeared, and Christian Europe, as it did with so many other pagan traditions, merely clothed it in Christian robes. Often when a witch was tried by water, the priest prayed over the water, recalled details of the Christian tradition, and thanked God just before they dunk the accused. One example from Germany:

May omnipotent God, who did order baptism to be made by water, and did grant remission of sins to men through baptism: may He, through His mercy, decree a right judgement through that water. If, namely, thou art guilty in that matter, may the water which received thee in baptism not receive thee now; if, however, thou art innocent, may the water which received thee in baptism receive thee now. Through Christ our Lord." [Kepler's Witch, p303]

Thus we see, with a woman's life hanging in the balance, our benevolent, all knowing and all powerful God responding to the prayer in exactly the same way as the totally unresponsive, ever silent, nonexistent god Baal responded. He didn't. At most witch trials, torture was used to obtain confessions and/or testimonials on the activity of other suspected witches. The torture used included chest compressions under heavy weights making breathing difficult, if not impossible. Partial drownings, pulling fingernails, branding irons, etc. were some of the additional tortures put to use by church officials. During all those centuries of untold crime, all in the name of enforcing "you shall not allow a witch to live" how did God let it be known what He is like? Did He let it be known where He stands on the issue of witch persecution? Even at this point in time some people persist in the belief that witches do exist. With an overwhelming majority utterly opposed to witch persecution, the religious extremists find it advantageous to remain silent about their suppressed wish to enforce God's law, that is, to kill witches. Has God yet spoken clearly on the issue?

We proceed to the crusades. With full backing of the Holy Roman Catholic Church, Europe armed itself, and marched on the Muslim's, ransacking, looting, and raping everywhere, along the way. Did God let it be known where He stood on that issue? The Catholic church sold indulgences to these crusaders and others offering forgiveness of sins yet to be committed in the future. Did God reveal His opinion on indulgences or was it a rebellious Catholic priest named Martin Luther who brought forward a dissenting opinion? Had God revealed clearly where he stood, the Thirty Years War may well not have happened. With the Reformation well under way, Catholic Spain made plans to attack England to end Protestantism by military might. Neither the Catholics nor the Protestants were given the benefit of a clear demonstration of where God stood on the issue. Armies stood across from one another, both fully convinced that God was on their side. And God chose not to enlighten them. When the Spanish Armada en route to demolish Protestantism ran into a powerful, destructive storm the English called it God's wind. You may well guess that the Spanish called it the devil's wind. We do not know who was right.

We must make a brief mention of the Inquisition. After the appetite for crusades waned in Europe, the Catholic Church turned its attention to heretics within its own ranks. If it made sense to attack the Muslims as enemies of the church, it made even more sense to attack those within its own ranks who promoted ideas the church did not agree with. A biblical basis for the persecution of heretics was very easy to find. "When a prophet or dreamer appears among you and offers you a sign or a portent and calls on you to follow other gods, whom you have not known, and worship them, even if the sign or portent should come true, do not listen to the words of that prophet or dreamer. God is testing you through him to discover whether you love the Lord your God with all your heart and soul. You must follow the Lord your God and fear him. You must keep his commandments and obey him, serve him and hold fast to him. That prophet or dreamer shall be put to death for he has preached rebellion against the Lord your God." [Deuteronomy 13:1-5] You must keep his commandments and then follows one such commandment: that rebellious (heretical) prophet is to be stoned, burned or hanged! Or they turned to Exodus 32:26-29 where Moses initiated the first extirpation of heresy. The Israelites, fearing that Moses was permanently gone, had Aaron make a god to help them; a golden bull calf was substituted for God Jehovah, a very jealous God. Moses was very angry. What to do? The Levites, declaring themselves to be "on the Lord's side," armed themselves and set out to "kill brother, friend and neighbor." Three thousand members of the opposition were liquidated. And by this action the Levites had "consecrated themselves to the Lord." Thus, the Inquisition was validated. Now it was the Holy Roman Catholic Church that set out to liquidate the opposition. And suffering and death was unleashed upon hundreds of thousands of people. One of the very darkest periods in the history of the Holy Roman Catholic Church unfolded. And there were God fearing, righteous, prayerful people, fully convinced that God was fully in support of the church's extirpation of heresy. God remained silent.

He also remained silent on the issue of slavery. Sincere religious leaders found themselves on opposite sides of the issue. Those in favour of slavery quoted many passages from the Holy Scriptures. "Slaves, you must obey your earthly masters. Show them great respect and be as loyal to them as you are to Christ. Try to please them at all times and not just when you think they are watching." [Ephesians 6:5-7 See also Colossians 3:22-25]. In consequence of God's refusal to inform the respective leaders of both sides as to where He stood on the issue, it ended up being settled on a battlefield. After the antislavery side won, most people assumed that God was against slavery.

By comparison to the previously discussed issues, the present issues are not nearly so bloody and replete with suffering. But they are not inconsequential issues. Can a practicing gay person be accepted as a person in good standing in a Christian church? Among the many laws and rulings given in Leviticus we read that homosexuality is an abomination. "If a man has intercourse with a man as with a woman, they both commit an abomination." [Leviticus 20:13] The Holy Scriptures then go onto specify the appropriate punishment – they shall be put to death. We note immediately that lesbians have, strangely, been exempted from this harsh proscription. Nothing is said about them. Further, we note that this heavy condemnation of male homosexuality must be set in the general context of Leviticus where we find many other rulings that we will have a difficult time agreeing with.

1) If any man reviles his parents, he shall be put to death. [Leviticus 20:9]

2) If a man commits adultery with his neighbor's wife, both shall be put to death. We note that Leviticus abounds with death penalties. [Leviticus 20:10]

3) "No man among your descendents for all time who has any physical defect … shall come up to the veil nor approach the altar … lest he … profane my sanctuary." [Leviticus 21:17-23]

4) "Whoever utters the name of the Lord shall be put to death … by stoning." [Leviticus 26:16]

5) `"Israelites shall not be sold as slaves are sold. … Such slaves as you have, male or female shall come from the nations round about you; from them you may buy slaves. You may also buy the children … as slaves … . These may become your property, and you may leave them to your sons after you. You may use them as slaves permanently. … An Israelite shall not have the status of a slave, he shall have the status of a hired labourer, and you shall not let him be driven with ruthless severity." [Leviticus 25:43-53] Does this appear to allow both ownership of non Israelite slaves and also the misery of driving them with ruthless severity?

Certainly then, in Leviticus at least, homosexuality gets a clear condemnation. We have had a profound change of heart on the issue of slavery as it is given in Leviticus. We have dared to overrule the official biblical approval of slavery as given by God to Moses [Leviticus 1:1] in Leviticus. Slavery has now become an abomination. Will we now see a similar profound change of heart on the issue of homosexuality as it is outlined in Leviticus? Will we dare to overrule the official biblical condemnation of homosexuality as an abomination? Will homosexuality now receive our non biblical official approval?

Again, we have fully sincere, prayerful "good" people on both sides of the issue. But both sides of the issue are agreed that God will not reveal where he stands. Does God continue to insist that women are to be silent in church or should it be permissible for women to become priests in the Holy Roman Catholic Church? Will God reveal where he stands on that issue?

We are left with just another heavy quandary. Why would God allow his most sincere followers to wallow about facing contentious issues? Despite their desperate plea to God "please let us know where you stand" he chooses to remain silent. As a consequence, horrendous crimes and suffering happen. And we are left hoping that the militarily successful side on a particular issue actually represents God's point of view.

A fifth cause of suffering in this world derives from the bedrock of biology. Life developed on this planet in the harshest possible circumstances. With the aid of an "intelligent designer" or without, the life that developed very quickly discovered a remarkable fact. A million cells found themselves all placed in the same savage, hostile environment but the million cells now discover that despite similar external appearance, their inner design harbours differences. Five hundred thousand cells succumb immediately in the harsh environment. Four hundred thousand die very soon, etc. But five of the original one million have the good fortune to be able to "make it." They manage to live, and not just live, they also manage to reproduce before the fundamental law of all life sweeps them away. From primitive cells to mankind: our days are numbered. And when the offspring of those five fortunate cells meet their environment, they find themselves much better equipped than the original one million cells to face that environment. They have been bequeathed with the superior DNA of the five cells, while the inferior DNA of the 999,995 cells, which inferiority rendered them incapable of sustaining their life, has been swept aside. This Charles Darwin called the "survival of the fittest." Seeing the similarities and differences between animals in, for example, the large family of mammals, Darwin began to see patterns and trends. A mammal living far from large bodies of water would derive no benefit from strong swimming capability. In fact, such a capability could become a disadvantage on land. But the mammal living close to large bodies of water might derive huge survival advantages from strong swimming capability. Thus one group had survivors that could run fast, and the second group had survivors that could swim fast. This Charles Darwin called evolution.

Thus we can see a very effective mechanism put in place by God (other people prefer to say mother nature) that has produced design, beauty, touch, smell and taste, the full fledged miracle of the life we see all around us and in ourselves. When we see a baby being born into this world, in particular one bequeathed with our own DNA, we cannot help but be wonderstruck. What a marvel of design. But we may not be clearly aware that this new life forms the most recent link in a chain of life containing exclusively, as we go backwards link by link, the superior DNA of the fittest previous links, that is, the DNA of the survivors. If the child is born with excellent eyesight, it will be because other links in the chain, that branch off to a side, while attached to your continuous chain, were dead-ended because their eyesight was inadequate. If the child is born with a fine brain, we find exactly the same reason. Sideways links attached to your chain were again dead ended because their brain was inadequate. Thus it becomes clear that we generally have fine brains because those links, while attached to our own continuous chain, which had inadequate brains, were not able to extend themselves forward. That portion of the chain at that link simply ended.

Can it be that these links in the chain are not really chain links at all? They are actually skin, blood, flesh, bones and emotion constituted human beings! We suddenly comprehend that "survival of the fittest" can be changed into "non survival of an unfit person". It can also be termed the "culling of the inferior". It means people whose inferiority causes nature to sweep them aside.

It is clear that we are all beneficiaries of that long selection process. It is good to be healthy, good looking and smart. However, these DNA gifts have come to us at a huge, horrific price. That price is of course all the dead ended links, those cursed with some major or minor defect in their DNA that rendered them less capable of survival and reproduction. It may be difficult to empathize with those dead-ended links if they occurred in the mists of long past times. Even grandparents begin to dissipate in that mist. Never-the-less, I am glad that my father's mother was healthy, good looking and smart, and that her DNA is in me instead of the DNA of her sister who died of a childhood disease which my grandmother survived. But sympathy or empathy for my grandmother's sister, the link that was to be dead ended? But when we see these dead ended links here, directly among us, among our loved ones, among our children, we can see suffering on a grand scale. And it becomes personal when some of us are forced to realize that it is myself that is destined to become a "dead-ended link."

It is one thing to be good looking, healthy and smart and make a decision to dead end ones DNA by having no offspring. It is a frequently made decision these days where the balance is struck between choosing a life of luxury, travel and professional pursuits, or a life of less money, luxury, travel, etc. but a long term commitment to family. With birth control options readily available the decision to not have a baby is pressed upon us. And many choose the life of luxury, travel and professional activities. Their DNA has been dead-ended. In this connection we know the derisive word "DINKS" standing for double income no kids. In years past to be a barren woman was the ultimate tragedy. Now we have gorgeous, very "sexy" women who avoid pregnancy at all costs. We need not extend any sympathy toward those who voluntarily choose to become dead end links.

But when we go to the hospitals and asylums and see those who have been deprived of a "normal" life, the tragedy and the suffering is impossible to overlook. And, of course, our history shows irregular intervals when the ravages of horrific diseases, and natural and cosmic disasters, laid many low. Each time the rule standing clearly stamped above all of us was "survival of the fittest." Were there exceptions? Of course! But can we detect the hand of God in providing the exceptions status? Not at all. Some of us managed to get lucky in that "tyranny of probability." Superior knowledge often did grant the exceptions status. During the Black Death plague in England, it was often observed that the pastors and priests, after making it clear that God was imposing a horrific disease on all of them for their past sins, would leave the city and their parishioners. They left the site of the dread disease and its means of spreading. Of course the parishioners died in large numbers, but the priests and pastors found themselves on the exemptions list. The city of Oberammergau in Germany took the unprecedented action of a total brutally enforced quarantine when news of the plague came to them. The gates were shut early enough. The disease had not and did not enter. The religious leaders chose, of course, to credit God with the miraculous exemption of their city from the disease. They instituted the Passion Plays, now famed around the world, to give thanks and glory to God for this miraculous intervention. Has anyone thought to ask why Oberammergau deserved and got God's exemption, but London did not?

When a baby is born the parents are in a state of excitement, dread and hope. One glance at the newly arrived infant shows so much. Firstly, is it alive? We wait desperately for that first vigorous wail telling us that the first breath had been taken. The face. Thankfully, both eyes are there. No abnormality that we can see. The back is straight. Ten fingers, ten toes. And the genitalia also qualifies as normal. We are overwhelmed with joy and thankfulness.

It does not always go that way. A baby gift pool was started at a place of employment for a very well liked pregnant young employee. Money was pooled in and whoever guessed most closely at the date of arrival, weight and gender of the baby would win $100.00 and the remaining money would become a baby gift. The baby was born with severe congenital defects and soon died. There were tears all around. And the money in the pool became a source of embarrassment.

We are all aware that not all babies are born endowed with all that is necessary for a "normal" life. Many of these have congenital defects that force them to become a dead end link. The pain and the suffering are untold. Why does God allow it to happen? Why has God imposed this rule upon us that not only shall the unfit also be born, but also that these unfit shall live a life, often characterized by incompetence, pain and an early demise? The Bible once again provides no solace. "Who do you think you are to question God? Does the clay have the right to ask the potter why he shaped it the way he did? Doesn't a potter have the right to make a fancy bowl or a plain bowl out of the same lump of clay?" [Romans 9:20-21] The sense of morality, ethics and benevolence that characterize this writer is not our sense. Making an ugly, leaky pot can in no way be compared to creating a baby with spina bifida. Does an ugly useless pot experience pain? Whether you are a creationist, Design by a Mind Theorist or an Evolutionist makes no difference. The pain and suffering stricken baby will be swept aside after a short pain laden life. He will become a dead-end link. The hidden brutal irony is that we are forced to acknowledge that our own good looks, health and brains has been achieved by dead ending all those with weak health, lopsided bodies and dull brains. God seems to have chosen a suffering and pain intensive means to provide a very positive end. Does the end justify the means?

A sixth cause of suffering in this world derives, as did the fifth, from the bedrock of biology. In the design that God, or mother nature, put in place, when life in all its various forms came into being, one uniform inexorable law was placed over all of them. Whether that life form was a virus, bacteria, worm, fish or human being, each one is born with an inbuilt, ineluctable, expiry process. For human beings and our pets, and farm animals, this expiry process has been studied endlessly by medical scientists, and of course, the veterinarians. We all seem to follow the same general pattern: growth first, we get stronger, faster and smarter, then a leveling off and then the aging process. The watchwords are weaker, slower and less smart. My son who has competed in medium to long distance races has kept track of his P.B.'s. These are, of course, his personal bests. The list has become quite long. While he was tracking his P.B.'s I was keeping an ad hoc listing in my mind of my P.W.s. These are, of course, my personal worsts. My son was advancing and I was declining.

The aging process proceeds sufficiently slowly for most of us that the month by month, year by year increments are hardly noticeable. Or we choose to ignore these rather uncomfortable facts. But the facts do surround us on all sides. Whether you are a teen, middle-aged or older, no one will dispute the ancient adage: life has two guarantees, death and taxes. Thus it is with surprise and disappointment that we read in McGraths's book <u>Suffering and God</u>: "God is obliged to bring about the funeral of this great myth - the myth of our personal immortality" [p33] and "Suffering strips away our illusions of immortality." [p33] Once again we disagree whole heartedly with McGrath. Whoever promoted or believed this illusion? What planet is he from!? Never-the-less, it is the privilege of youth to be so far removed from the expiry process that they give it scant attention. It is like a young smoker being told that his/her habit may well result in lung cancer or throat cancer or prostate cancer, etc. But when we tell that young smoker that the penalty may happen in thirty years, it becomes an empty threat. It <u>may</u> happen? And, if it does, it will take thirty or more years? But time does pass. And the curse of nicotine will arrive at some point and collect its dues. Youth will continue to be lost on youth. But, if you have the good fortune to advance in age, the value of youth will yet be made clear to you.

Let us proceed to the heart of the matter. Let us visit an old folks home. Here is an old pastor from a Mennonite church. His sphincters do not close anymore. He is diapered. He is almost totally blind. He suffers from senile dementia but has random semi-lucid moments. The clear message from him during those moments is his wish to die. His brain cannot retrieve any memory of salvation, Christ's message, or a heavenly reward. Just deliver me from my humiliations and my suffering. It is in no way a pretty picture.

Complaints about the pain of the aging process are largely muted. In fact, it has been a difficult choice for me to include it here as a major source of suffering. However, everyone agrees that it is, in fact, a major cause of suffering. Why the muting? The facts of life are the facts of life and to complain about them seems both futile and even stupid. Do we complain that rocks are hard? That you can't breathe under water? That we can't fly? But when we stand beside the pain racked body of an aged loved one, who has just slipped and fallen, we have to ask "God, why?" In addition to osteoarthritis, this old lady has osteoporosis. Due to the fall she now has a broken elbow and a broken hip.

Can the Bible help us? The infirmities of old age are very rarely mentioned. Senile dementia does not exist in the Bible. Nor does osteoporosis. They seem to have been aware of decreased sexual and reproductive functioning with older age. Abraham "laughed and said to himself 'can a son be born to man who is one hundred years old' " [Genesis 17:17] And Sarah laughed to herself (ninety years old) and said "I am past bearing children." [Genesis 18:12] Never-the-less, she does become pregnant and bears the son Isaac. It is with astonishment that we read that

Abraham subsequently married another wife in addition to having concubines. Without the aid of Viagra, at an age in excess of 100, and having laughed at the possibility of impregnating Sarah, he now goes on to have six more sons by his new wife Keturah. [Genesis 25:1-3] He died "at a good old age after a very long life and was gathered to his father's kin." [Genesis 25:8-9] We have no indication of the infirmities of old age whatever. What we do see with Abraham is a lovely sense of humor, a somewhat lowered level of certainty that his reproductive gear would work only to find that it worked superbly, repeatedly!

But our present facts remain as they are. And when we are faced with those infirmities of old age among our loved ones and then have to confront them personally, the question will arise "Why God?" Why indeed this horrific pre death suffering? Are these to be viewed as final tests from God? And if we fail that test and I reach the conclusion that God is not benevolent; we will be consigned to hell. Or is this suffering a final dose of punishment for previous sins?

When that pre death suffering and humiliation tests us beyond our power to endure, many people's thoughts turn to suicide or even assisted suicide. Or we simply disconnect the life support systems. Or simply make the firm decision to stop eating. It is difficult to find God's role in all this. In this area of strong contentious opinion we will note, as before, that God chooses to remain silent.

Perhaps, in addition to the previously mentioned suffering that derives from our biology, we should also mention the extreme pain that we encounter when our women give birth. Thanks to our generally effective medical interventions, we now have less reason to be afraid of the complications of childbirth. But a visit to any older cemetery will show us how many women died in childbirth. When the diagnosis was brought in that there was a breach presentation, or the head of the baby exceeds the size of the pelvic opening, everyone knew that the long excruciating labor may well end in the death of both mother and child. Where is was possible to save either the mother or the child, but not both, the Holy Roman Catholic Church ruled that the child would be given precedence. Unbelievably brutal caesarean sections were performed. At times when the birth itself went normally, "kind bett fieber" (German for child bed fever) would ensue. The infection was often fatal. Finally, a doctor by the name of Semmelweiss discovered, and successfully promoted, sterile techniques and this type of infection very nearly vanished. The facts remain that now, but more often in the past, people would have to stand by the expectant mother-to-be to witness the usual very intense labor pains to be rewarded with a beautiful, healthy baby, or, tragically, to witness intense suffering to be ended by a death or even a double death. The question why has been and will be raised.

A final and seventh cause for suffering derives from this statement by God: "For I, the Lord your God, am a jealous God. I punish the children for the sins of the fathers, to the third and fourth generations." [Exodus 20:57] OR "Jehovah the Lord, a God compassionate and gracious, long suffering ever constant and true … forgiving iniquity rebellion and sin … but one who punishes sons and grandsons to the third and fourth generation for the iniquity of their fathers." [Exodus 34:6-7] OR "The Lord … who forgives iniquity … and punishes sons to the third and fourth generation for the iniquity of their fathers." OR " … a jealous God. I punish the children for the sins of the fathers to the third and fourth generations …" [Deuteronomy 5:9-10]

The writer again has a sense of ethics and godly "perfection" that seems entirely foreign to us. A sinful ancestor will unleash god's punishment upon an utterly innocent child, or grand child. It is completely alien to our sense of justice, but we are forced to see it written, not once, but four times. Nothing would seem more unjust to us than to visit the punishment due to a sinner upon a totally innocent great-great-grandchild. Twice it is mentioned that God will "keep faith with thousands (of generations) with those who love me and keep my commandments." [Deuteronomy 5:10] Does this blessing from our righteous ancestors take precedence over the punishment coming to us due to sinful ancestors? Do we have any ancestors of whom it may be said that they loved God and kept His commandments? Is it sufficient to keep some of the commandments some of the time? My ancestors tried to love God, and tried, often unsuccessfully, to keep the commandments. Am I to be punished or blessed? Or is the curse of punishment to the third and fourth generations to be simply disregarded, swept under the rug? Are we allowed to do that to any passage from Holy Scriptures?

We have examples in the Bible where punishment due to a father, King David, was deferred to his offspring. We remember the story of David. From the top of his palace, he spots a very beautiful woman, Bathsheba, bathing herself on a roof top in full view of himself. Her plan to seduce the king works. She is brought to the king and the heat of their desire is satisfied. She conceives. David knew she was a married woman, so he now issues orders that her soldier husband be brought home that he might have sex with Bathsheba, that he might believe that he was the true father of the conceived child. Her husband refuses sex with his wife. And when he is sent back into battle he is ordered into harms way and is killed. King David adds Bathsheba to his large harem. And a son was born. Nathan, the prophet, makes it clear that what David had done was wrong. In consequence of that grievous sin many curses are laid upon David. These punishments include "you shall not die but, because you have shown contempt for the Lord, the boy that has been born to you shall die." [2 Samuel 12:14] David's iniquity resulted in the Lord striking the young boy with a severe illness. Despite David's prayers and fasting, the boy died on the seventh day. It is difficult for us to see any justice at all in the wailing, innocent baby boy with a disease inflicted directly by God, finally breathing his last because the father had sinned.

In the New Testament in the gospel of John we read: Jesus' disciples asked, "Teacher why was this man born blind? Was it because he or his parents sinned?" [John 9:2] Here we hear the disciples second guessing what Jesus' answer to the question would be. They are aware of the Old Testament quotations. In their minds it is quite possible that this unfortunate man was born blind due to the iniquity of some ancestor. It offends us that they could think that possible. It also offends us to think that the second plausible cause for his blind at birth affliction was in consequence of a sin he was yet to perpetrate in the future! Born blind because of a sin that he would commit when he was, perhaps, thirty years of age!? We are very pleased to read that Christ rejects both of those options. We have previously discussed Christ's answer to their question. We would have preferred Jesus to say that no child would ever again be punished for the iniquity of one or more ancestors. But he did not. God's statement that He will punish innocent children to the third and fourth generation for the iniquity of their fathers, that statement is still in effect.

We are pleased to note that the bible makes no mention whatever of the iniquity of mothers resulting in punishment by God on the children. Bathsheba is in no way implicated by Nathan in the wrong doing. Her seduction of King David is not worthy of mention by Nathan. She is not mentioned as praying and fasting for the afflicted boy. She is simply just another insignificant female in Nathan's mind. It was the sin of the father that induced God to punish the child, not the sin of the mother. Is this just another dimension of gender discrimination?

Epilogue to Suffering

Polio was a painful, debilitating and sometimes fatal childhood disease. I used the past tense word "was" because it was in 1955 that the announcement was heard around the world that the Salk vaccine worked. It was one of those landmarks of the twentieth century that stand out like a snow-capped mountain peak against blue sky. Instead of another act of evil, with unprecedented numbers of people butchered, we have an event where science effectively removed what was thought to be an unavoidable scourge. Millions benefited. It was not easy. The challenge before our medical scientists was daunting. It is a powerful and emotional experience to don their clothes, shoes, minds and hearts to journey down that path leading to a cessation of the ravages of that horrific disease. Many books can be recommended including Patenting the Sun by J. S. Smith.

In the context of this book it is the contrast between the scientific approach to polio and the Christian theology approach to polio. The theologians had no difficulty at all explaining the disease polio. They, of course, never got enmeshed or lost in the complexities of bacteriology or virology. No need for statistical analysis as to where and when and to whom the disease attached itself. No need to hypothesize and then run the scientific tests to verify the hypothesis. Does it bear out under scientific scrutiny? No need to propose and test a vastly complex and expensive solution strategy. No need to consider the possibility of being wrong. For the theologians, the question why was answered as follows: 1) The afflicted person had sinned and as per Deuteronomy 28:15 to 68, God was punishing that person for his sin. And in God's wisdom the punishment was to take the form of affliction with polio. 2) The afflicted person was being tested by God, or a caregiver or loved one in the polio victim's circle of friends was to be tested as per biblical quotations like "… in order to test him" [2 Chronicles 32:31] And God in his wisdom decided to test that someone by afflicting someone with polio. 3) A male ancestor(s) had sinned and God's undertaking to punish the children to the third and fourth generation was being enforced. And in God's wisdom, the best way to enforce that punishment was to afflict some unfortunate progeny with polio.

The only real difficulty the theologian encountered was choosing one of the three cited reasons as the primary reason. Or, more simply, all three were equally effective ingredients. And, of course, the solution: no more sinning! And nobody thought to ask "even with no sinning whatever, might God not still test us by inflicting polio!?"

The Christian theologians contributed nothing to bringing the miraculous Salk vaccine into being. Indeed they put road blocks in the path of the scientists. How dare you even think that you can somehow derail God's imposition of punishment or testing? As in much earlier times when the scientists wished to unravel the secret inner workings of the human body, the church officials were there to curse them and to prevent the dissection of cadavers. Or the early European immigrants to America, dying of scurvy, saved by medications from the pagan aboriginals, with the priests and pastors issuing glory, worship and adulation to God for curing them.

Now that polio is cured (perhaps only temporarily) our present day theologians will studiously avoid any pronouncements from predecessor theologians on the dread disease. With polio removed from the arsenal of weapons with which to punish or test, what will God do? It is clear, the children, in western societies, under the care of scientific medical experts, are healthier and live longer than any previous generation of children. Are we to conclude that God has experienced a change of heart, that he now is less willing to punish and to test? Or is there room in our minds and hearts to reach other conclusions?

# Chapter 6
# Holy Scriptures: Preferred Passages?

**Preferred Passages?**

At this point it appears that Predestination, like the Ransom Theory of Atonement, belongs in the trash bin of grievous theological errors. In the 18th century John Wesley attacked the theory of Predestination. His attack left Predestination fatally injured. However, we will take note here of the fact that the denunciations of Predetermination take the form of common sense; this standing in contrast to finding that the Bible provides no evidence or support of Predestination. Can a God characterized as benevolent, determine his small handful of preferred people, his Elect, according to his "good pleasure" and "divine will?" These he loved. But those that he did not love, the greater part of mankind, those not chosen and not elected by God, those he preordained to damnation. The majority of all people thus have absolutely no opportunity for salvation. Our hackles are raised immediately. Our sense of justice is appalled and revolted. Thus common sense has ruled that Predestination is in violation of everything we cherish in the Christian faith. Then how did Predestination ever make it into the Christian faith? Was it ever actually a part of the Christian faith? It certainly was! And amazingly, it certainly is!

When people are baptized or confirmed into membership in a particular Christian church, they are required to give a statement of their beliefs. They must confirm that they are in agreement with the basic beliefs of the Holy Roman Catholic Church or the Presbyterian Church or the Alliance or Baptist Church. Should you choose to become baptized as a member of a Baptist Church, you should become familiar with the New Hampshire confession which most Baptists presently adhere to. Article nine reads: "We believe that election is the eternal purpose of God." The Southern Baptist states it differently. [Baptist Faith and Message 1963] "Election is the gracious purpose of God … and is infinitely wise, holy and unchangeable." Very similarly, in the Reformed confession, we find "Election is the unchangeable purpose of God by which, before the foundation of the world, according to the most free pleasure of his will and of his mere grace, out of mankind he hath chosen in Christ, a set number of certain men." We have to remind ourselves that if some have been preordained by God - have been elected by God - to be the Elect, others, the majority were, by default, appointed to unavoidable damnation.

The Anglican Church in article 18 of their confession it states: "Predestination to life is the everlasting purpose of God … to deliver from curse and damnation those whom he hath chosen, in Christ, out of mankind."

Martin Luther stated "It was preordained who should receive the word of life, and who should disbelieve it, who should be delivered from their sins and who should be hardened in them."

Finally, Augustine, a preeminent theologian of the Holy Roman Catholic Church stated: "Concerning predestination God formed, before the creation of the world, the resolution to redeem certain men to Christ and apply to them his grace. Concerning these, there is a strictly definite number. Only to the elect does the effectual call come. All therefore, rests in the hands of God and the call of his choice."

Why would so many (at one time all) theologians of all different Christian faiths subscribe to the idea of predestination? These theologians were as sincere as they could be, they were prayerful, they were as motivated as the best presently are to understand God's work, and to live a God-fearing life. They did not invent the idea. They studied God's word, they immersed themselves in the Holy Scriptures and found it there in countless quotations. If you should have the desire to study biblical predestination in detail, you can do so by contacting Bible Study Time Inc. PO Box 1714, Spartanburg, SC, 29304, phone (864) 585-0470, Dr. W. R. Crews. Here it will suffice to include the following:

1) "Before the world was created God chose us to live with him to be his holy and innocent and loving people." [Ephesians 1:4]

2) "God hath from the beginning chosen you to salvation." [2 Thessalonians 2:93]

3) "It has been granted to you [we understand the Elect] to know the secrets of the kingdom of heaven; but to those others [we understand the non Elect] it has not been granted. For the man who has [part of the Elect] will be given more till he has enough and to spare; and the man who has not will forfeit even what he has." [Matthew 13:11-12]

4) "To you the secret of the kingdom of God has been given, but to those who are outside [we understand the non-Elect] everything comes by way of parables so that, as the Scripture says, they may look and look but see nothing, they may hear and hear, but understand nothing; otherwise they might turn to God and be forgiven." [Mark 4:11-12]

5) "The man who has will be given more and the man who has not will forfeit even what he thinks he has." [Luke 8:18]

6) "Elect according to the foreknowledge [foreordination in the original Greek] of God the father." [1 Peter 1:2]

How could so many theologians for so many centuries hold on to the idea of predestination? How could they not? The idea of predestination involves dividing people into two categories, the Elect and the damned.

Our theological ancestors were very, very familiar with similar divisions of mankind into two categories, one privileged the other disadvantaged. Thus we see, in the Old Testament, an immediate and powerful division: they, the Israelites, were the privileged, the chosen people. And the people around them, in particular the Egyptians and then the seven tribes to be annihilated, were the disadvantaged. Those theologians were entirely at peace with the biblical fact of the very small group of privileged chosen people. And the biblical fact of the disadvantaged non chosen people. "At midnight I will go out among the Egyptians. Every first born in the land of Egypt shall die: the first born of the Pharaoh who sits on his throne, the first born of the slave-girl at the hand mill, and all the first born of all the cattle. All Egypt will send up a great cry of anguish, a cry the like of which has never been heard before nor ever will be again. But among Israel not a dog's tongue shall be so much as scratched." [Exodus 11:4-7] Our feeling of justice and benevolence will be greatly offended by the treatment of the Egyptians versus that of the Israelites. But our theological ancestors were quite at peace with God's choices: the chosen and the damned.

Next we see the Old Testament's very easy and unconcerned acceptance of slavery. Mankind simply divided up into free people and not free people. This was seen to be as much the natural order of things as was the division of mankind into male and female. It was natural justice that slaves would obey just as men would dominate over women. Any question of justice here? Our theological forbears could discern no injustice whatever. Then predestination. Again we have mankind herded into two camps, the privileged and the disadvantaged: the Elect and the damned. It constituted no problem. The feudal system had two categories, the aristocracy and the bottom end masses, and of course, the church officials. All around them, those theologians had mankind divided into the two camps. And they were aware of the statements from Esdras: "You made this world for our sake, and the rest of all nations descended from Adam are nothing, they are no better than spittle." [2 Esdras 6:55-57] "But I shall not grieve for the many who are lost; they are no more than a vapor." [2 Esdras 7:61] In this context those theologians had no difficulty with predestination as just another division of all people into two camps.

The Anglican Church of the 1700's was an elitist organization. Most members of it were quite convinced that they had been predestined to membership in that wonderful club called the Elect. Most were like-wise convinced that the masses were predestined to membership in the "other club." John Wesley loved preaching. From the sermon on the mount, he deduced that preaching need not be confined inside any building. Further he deduced that preaching need not be only to the small number of the Elect. His audiences were huge and his appeal was electric. Wesley then had to confront the question: does it make sense to preach to the non Elect? Does it make sense that anyone should be disbarred from an opportunity for salvation? He attacked, denounced, and destroyed the doctrine of predestination.

What to do with the biblical quotations that contained predestination? Reinterpretations were (and are) attempted but the text is too blunt and clear. Therefore, the solution to be favored was one of de-emphasis. The text stayed as it was but the pages to be studied, or lovingly fingered, changed. Mankind had changed, the French Revolution was in the wind and government by the people for the people had been conceived. The masses arrogating to themselves the power of the masters!? The unheard of was being spoken and thought about. Slavery came to the considered unjust. And preordaining the masses to damnation? Repugnantly and repulsively impossible!

The bible cannot be rewritten. We are aware that it has indeed been rewritten but we will assume those "rewritten" scriptures to be of negligible significance. And when the ethics of this book collide with the ethics of the new world, with its empowered masses, our present day theologians really have no choice but to studiously ignore the offending scriptural passages. Thus, in effect, we have expungements. So it comes as no surprise that even evangelists will announce "That (which you have quoted) is <u>not</u> in the bible!" But when a bible is found and that particular translation is validated, it is found with dismay that it is indeed in the bible.

Here is a partial list of those expungements.

1) All those quotations that directly or indirectly involve predestination.

2) "Just as the Lord took delight in you, prospering and increasing you, so now it will be his delight (other editions state "he will rejoice") to destroy and exterminate you." [Deuteronomy 28:63] It has become unacceptable for God to rejoice when he inflicts suffering on man. As we have seen, modern theologians much prefer to have God suffering with us.

3) "No, my friends, do not be so wicked. Look I have two daughters, both virgins; let me bring them out to you, and you can do what you like with them; but do not touch these men, because they have come under the shelter of my roof." [Genesis 19:8] Lot, the father of the two virgins had been judged by God's representatives to be a good man. And this good man was prepared to hand over his virgin daughters to the sex crazed thugs

and sadists who had surrounded his house.

4) "Bring out the man who has gone into your house for us to have intercourse with him. … No, my friends, do nothing so wicked. … Here is my daughter, a virgin, let me bring her out to you. Rape her and do to her what you please; but you shall not commit such an outrage against this man. … The Levite took hold of his concubine and thrust her outside for them." [Judges 19:22-26] Is there a more heinous offense that a man can commit against a daughter or against a wife? And the Bible presents the two men presiding over the lives of this daughter and this wife as good men. It is too much!

5) Any man who has physical defect "shall not come up to the Veil nor approach the altar because he has a defect in his body. Thus he shall not profane my sanctuary." [Leviticus 21:23] The defects are actually listed: blind, lame, stunted, overgrown, deformed, damaged testicle … etc. At a time when we do our utmost to assist those who suffer from some handicap, this quotation simply won't go down. Further we now clearly recognize that most people have one or more concealed handicaps. And those handicaps (concealed or visible) in no way diminish other strengths and talents. A ruling from God that a handicapped man shall not approach the altar because it would profane his sanctuary? No, it cannot be. Item 21, page 142, gives God, the potter, the right to shape humans in any way he wishes. But here he indicates that if he made you with a physical defect you shall not approach the altar lest you "profane my sanctuary."

6) "Pharaoh will let the Israelites out of his country, but I will make him stubborn." Does God interfere in the heart and mind of a man, in a leadership position, to change that man into a more evil man? In consequence of God's interference with the mind of the Pharaoh, how many people died horribly? Is it not Satan that has the job of interfering with a view to make man more evil? Due to Pharaoh's God induced stubbornness, every first born creature, man and animal alike, were made to die. God himself [Exodus 11:4-7] went out among all the Egyptians to kill them. If God had chosen not to interfere against the Pharaoh, if indeed he had chosen to soften his heart [Exodus 11:3] no action against the Egyptians would have been necessary. Is it possible to have God behave like Satan?

7) This is what is appointed for them who served the most high. Their reward is this: … "Their second joy is to see the souls of the wicked wandering ceaselessly, and the punishment in store for them." [2 Esdras V89-93] Here we have a description of the saved virtuous souls. They are presented as compassionless monsters, taking pleasure and joy from the prospect of heavy punishment for all those not saved. Is it possible to be a

Sister Teresa on earth with compassion for everyone, and once in heaven, take compassionless pleasure in the suffering of the damned? In Revelations we see a similar eagerness among the saved to savor the joy of seeing the damned suffer: "They gave a great cry: 'How long, sovereign Lord, holy and true, must it be before thou wilt vindicate us and avenge our blood on the inhabitants of the earth?" [Revelations 6:10]

8) "When a prophet or dreamer appears among you and calls on you to follow other Gods … that prophet shall be put to death, for he has preached rebellion against the Lord." [Deuteronomy 13:1-5] To live at peace with other people we must learn the lesson of tolerance. And we must accept the fact that other people worship other Gods (hopefully similar to our God) and worship in ways foreign to ours. Cultural diversity is a fact of life. To resent that diversity is counter productive. To advocate the killing of missionaries (ours to be killed by them, and theirs to be killed by us) is insanity. And to kill those who dare to think and dare to criticize that all powerful church elite: that would return us to the Inquisition and the Dark Ages. The Old Testament's readiness to impose the death penalty is repulsive.

9) "They put everyone to the sword, men, women, children … ." [Joshua 6:21] "They killed every living thing in it and wiped them all out … they put them to the sword as Moses, the servant of the Lord, had commanded." [Joshua 11:11-12] "So Joshua massacred the population of the whole region … he left no survivor, destroying everyone who drew breath as the Lord, the God of Israel, had commanded. Joshua carried the slaughter … on to Gaza and the whole land of Goshen and … ." [Joshua 10:40-41] We have here killing, wiping out, massacring, annihilating of people on a grand scale all at the command of the God of the Israelites, the unchanging God of Christianity.. The 20th century saw similar activity but the instigators of these crimes against humanity, genocide, and war crimes are now uniformly seen as thugs, sadists and monsters. They are allied not with God. If they were allied with any supernatural forces it was Satan who guided their efforts.

10) "I will make my arrows drunk with blood, my sword shall devour flesh, blood of slain and captives, the heads of the enemy princes." [Deuteronomy 32:41-42] Is this a God of love, mercy, forgiveness and justice that Moses describes in this passage? Or is it a God of anger, wrath, jealousy and blood lust? A warlord who behaves exactly like other warlords of the world before Moses, with Joshua, and through to the 20th century? A warlord who massacres and annihilates? Does an all powerful, all knowing

and benevolent God have to use weaponry and blood lust to accomplish his ends? Would it not be preferable to shape our history and progress not with swords and guns and killing technologies but with signs and miracles and gentle persuasion? Why harden hearts and minds if they can just as easily be softened and opened to accommodate the desperately desired peaceful solution?

11) "They have taken women of these nations as wives for themselves ... and so the holy race has been contaminated. ... We have committed an offence against our God in marrying foreign wives, daughters of the foreign population. ... Let us pledge ourselves to God to dismiss all these women and their brood, according to your advice, my Lord." [Ezra 9:1 to 10:3] We have seen horrific excesses of racism in the 20th century under the leadership of what we believe to have been Satanic monsters. To see racist concepts - a holy race being contaminated - and a wholesale dismissal of these contaminating women and their "brood" under the leadership of the Lord God of the Israelites, our unchanging Christian God, is devastating.

12) Solomon had 700 wives and 300 concubines." [Kings 11:2-4] "Solomon was devoted to them and loved them dearly." "They enticed him to serve other Gods." Is it possible to dearly love 1000 women? Is this to be read as an endorsement of polygamy, Solomon being blessed by God with "wisdom and insight and understanding as wide as the sand on the seashore?" Was Solomon really "wiser than any man?" [1 Kings 4:29-31] Polygamy is now unacceptable to us. Wisdom cannot happen in the context of rampant polygamy. A harem of 1000 women is more than a little disgusting. Wisdom cannot happen in the context of 1000 women imprisoned in their harem quarters.

13) "Cursed be Canaan slave of slaves shall he be to his brothers." [Genesis 9:25] Noah had just planted a vineyard, harvested grapes, made wine and gotten drunk. He lay naked in his tent. His son Ham happened to come into his father's tent, and crime of crimes, sin of sins, he saw his father's genitalia! Therefore, his son Canaan was cursed as we have read. Were other people also cursed to be slaves? The people occupying the promised land were to be annihilated. Those close by were not necessarily to be annihilated; these were eligible to become slaves. The New Testament encourages slaves to work hard for their masters even when the master is not watching. We now find slavery utterly unacceptable.

14) "Thou shalt not suffer a witch to live." This has been adequately addressed earlier. It is totally unacceptable to a modern Christian. The history of the Christian churches persecution of witches is depressing, tragic and deplorable.

15) "To you the secret of the kingdom of God has been given, but to those who are outside, everything comes by way of parables so that (as the scripture says) they may look and look but see nothing; they may hear and hear but understand nothing; otherwise they might turn to God and be forgiven." [Mark 4:10-12] Parables used to confuse and obfuscate!? Wildly impossible! Those on the outside must stay outside? This quotation is grossly dismaying. It is best if we pretend it doesn't exist.

16) "The man answered "My name is 'Lots" because I have lots of evil spirits. ... "Over on the hillside, 2000 pigs were feeding. So the evil spirits begged Jesus send us into those pigs. ... The whole herd rushed down a steep bank and drowned." [Mark 5:9-13] Where did all the evil spirits go after the 2000 pigs all drowned? Few people of faith today believe in devils and evil spirits. Does anyone believe in an incubus, an evil spirit or demon that appears on earth, to lay upon a woman during her sleep to have sex with her? The Holy Roman Catholic Church was convinced that Martin Luther was conceived by an incubus that snuck himself upon his sleeping mother. Does anyone believe in a succubus, an evil spirit or demon in female form that wiggles underneath to have sex with men in their sleep? Priests believed that their sinful dreams and nocturnal emissions proved the existence of succubi. These things belong in the past. And to exorcise demons from a human and send them into pigs? And the pigs go insane? And forget how to swim? The story is totally ludicrous. And yet, we read Christ's first empowerment listed at the end of Mark. "Everyone who believes in me will force out demons" in his name. Demon possession and exorcism are unacceptable to almost all Christians today.

17) "They will handle snakes and drink poison and not be hurt." [Mark 16:18] This is regarded by almost everyone as erroneous. Some primitive people in the backwoods (or swamps) of the Southern United States are reported as taking this quotation seriously. It is certainly an easy empowerment to test. The results are likewise easy to predict.

18) "Stay away from the Gentiles, and don't go to any Samaritan town. Go only to the people of Israel." [Matthew 10:5-6] Can it be that Jesus' message was only for the chosen people? Can it be that Christ changed his mind about the Gentiles right after his crucifixion? Can the all knowing Christ have a change of mind? It is unacceptable.

19) "I promise you that some of those standing here will not die before they see the Son of Man coming with his kingdom." [Matthew 16:28] [see also Matthew 24:34; Mark 13:30; Luke 9:27; Luke 21:32] Everyone was interested to know when Christ would return "with his kingdom."

Assuming adults standing there with him at a minimum age of 18 years, and assuming that the one to live the longest is the youngest, and will die at 100 years of age, Christ would have had to come back in a maximum of 82 years forward from the date when Jesus made the statement. Christ himself made the statement. And he told his favorite disciple that he was among those who would still be alive when Christ would return. The ending to the Gospel of John, termed enigmatic, is not enigmatic at all. The other disciples felt somewhat disadvantaged when the unconfirmed rumour circulated that the favorite, the most loved disciple of Jesus, was to be favored: he would live to see Christ returning with his kingdom. Would the others likewise live to see his return? Therefore, Peter asked "Lord, what about him?" Jesus knew immediately what the question was about. Jesus answered, "What is it to you if I want him to live until I return?" [John 21:20-23] It is extremely unsettling to read this quotation from the Holy Scriptures. About 2000 years have passed since Christ gave the date of his return. Is anyone from that crowd still alive?

20) "I have made thy name known to the men whom thou didst give me out of the world. They were thine, thou gavest them to me … I pray for them, I am <u>not</u> praying for the world but for those whom thou hast given me." [John 17:6-9] There are clear overtones of predestination here. Is Christ really interested only in those men that God gave him out of the world? What about the rest?

21) "Who do you think you are to question God? Does the clay have the right to ask the potter why he shaped it the way he did? Doesn't a potter have the right to make one vessel for beauty, distinction and honour and another for menial or ignoble or dishonourable use?" [<u>K.J.V. Amplified Holy Bible</u>. Romans 9:20-21] We have no objection whatever if it is unfeeling soulless pots that you are creating. If it is humans that you are creating that can feel pain and pleasure, that God, we hope, loves more than pots, he does <u>not</u> have the right to form misshapen, ignoble, defective human beings. And if it is contended that he has that right, he will still be unwilling ever to do so because he is benevolent. To view God as a potter, shaping some weak; some strong, some with eyes, some without; some with a straight, strong back, some with spina-bifida, with as little emotional attachments to his humans as a potter with a beautiful pot, or with an ugly pot, which he just smashed into the corner junk heap, this is deeply distressing. We are not pots!

22) "Now I want you to know that Christ is the head over all men, and a man is the head over a woman." "Men were created to be like God and to bring honour to God. … Women were created to bring honour to men. It

was the woman who was made from a man and not the man who was made from a woman. He was not created for her. She was created for him." [Corinthians 11:3-9] Women of the western world have been engaged in a long and sometimes bitter struggle for emancipation. They were aware of the end of the privileged, chosen status of the chosen people, the aristocracy, and the master class. That is, Gentiles became eligible for salvation in addition to Jews; the business class and trade guilds and the masses forced their way into the halls of power; the masters saw their slaves emancipated. Slaves empowered themselves to rise above the level of their previous masters. Why should the curse God addressed to Eve go on forever: "Your husband shall dominate over you." [Genesis] "When God's people meet in church, the women must not be allowed to speak. They must keep quiet and listen." [Corinthians 4:33-36] Women "should learn by being quiet and paying attention. They should be silent and not allowed to teach or to tell men what to do. After all, Adam was created before Eve and the man Adam was not the one who was fooled. It was the woman Eve who was completely fooled and sinned. But women will be saved by having children." If you believe these quotations to be acceptable to modern Christians, I will leave it in your hands to present them to the next meeting of Job's Daughters. You will not escape with your bodily and mental functions intact. But if you do perhaps you will have the courage to present also Amos 4:1-3:

> Women of Samaria
> you cows of Bashan …
> Who say to your lords
> "Bring drink for us!"
> The Lord God has sworn …
> They shall drag you away with hooks … fish hooks:
> You shall be cast in the mire.

It is astonishing that the Holy Roman Catholic Church still fully disbars all females from certain duties and functions. It is safe to say that many Roman Catholic women are extremely anxious to expunge the given quotations.

23) "Only God can give authority to anyone and he puts these rulers in their places of power. People who oppose the authorities are opposing what God has done and they will be punished. … They are God's servants." [Romans 13:1-4] The 20th century has been replete with evil governments. Thugs and sadists and their gangs have unsurped power. They have ruled supreme instituting reigns of terror. Millions died at the hands of those

monsters. Anyone who resisted was subjected to the terror of disappearing at midnight never to be heard from again. God assigned these monsters the authority to govern? If any supernatural assistance came to those monsters, it came from the devil. God put Stalin in his place of power? To oppose Hitler is to oppose God? It is beyond all sense and reason. It cannot be. It is a great relief to see that our theological leaders proceed from the premise that Romans 13:1-4 simply do not exist: they have been expunged.

24) "You have heard people say 'love your neigbours and hate your enemies. But I tell you to love your enemies and pray for anyone who mistreats you." [Matthew 5:43-44 also Mark 6:27-30] Which western Christian nation loves its enemies? In the United States we see on the currency, "In God We Trust". This nation bristles with military might and is, of course, prepared to demonstrate its willingness to use force. Thus, the military has its ironic sayings: "Praise the Lord and pass the ammunition!" OR "We love our enemies, especially when they are dead!" Instead of loving our enemies we kill our enemies. And we are agreed, that, at least in some situations, it was the right thing to do to terminate those enemies. It seems that present day Christians are quite capable of living with the total intellectual dissonance. Yes, we do love our enemies, and, yes, we will kill them! It surely makes no sense to love your enemies. At any time, when the "good" people in power lay down their arms, the thugs and sadists are absolutely guaranteed to come forward to take up the laid down weaponry and initiate another reign of terror. You don't even have to go so far as to lay down your arms and announce love for the enemies. Just a few less vigilant moments and the evil ones will find an opportunity to advance to a position of greater power. All their energy, brains and ambition are directed to that "holy grail" - power. They know that with power everything else comes automatically. Money, influence and even respect. And the most beautiful women of the world will extend their tender tentacles of sweet seduction toward them. Just like Bathsheba, these women invariable aim for those at or near the pinnacle of the power pyramid.

If the "good" people in power are not prepared to use the threat or actuality of military force, they will be immediately replaced by "evil" people. Power will pass from the "good" people to the "evil" people. We know that nothing can be worse. Therefore, the actuality here is that the injunction to love your enemies constitutes full fledged insanity. The reality is a complicated one: "good" people in power for too long will become corrupted. "Good" people in power seem capable of initiating military action with perhaps enriching the "military industrial complex" included as a not insignificant motivator. But love your enemies? If you love freedom and justice you cannot love those who would deprive you of freedom and justice. If you define your enemies as those who would undermine your freedom and justice, you cannot ever love them. Loving your enemies would become fatally misguided idealism. It might work if among the human race there are absolutely none that harbour potential for becoming thugs and sadists. If we are convinced that such potentialities exist within some of us, then we must keep the "good" in power. Any may the "good" absolutely never "love the enemy".

How do we apply Christ's injunction to love your enemy in the context of the Old Testament? When you and your ancestors have lived in your fertile, lovely place called home since time immemorial and then rumours start that a barbarian, warlike and ruthless tribe is approaching, panic begins to set in. Your spies report that this tribe is countless in numbers and has never been defeated. They are approaching your homeland. They have the immediate, direct, stated and avowed objective of taking for themselves the "fine cities which you did not build, houses full of good things which you did not provide, rock hewn cisterns which you did not hew, and vineyards and olive groves which you did not plant." [Deuteronomy 6:11-12] Who built these cities and houses, who hewed the cisterns and who planted the vineyards and olive groves? You did. It so happens, unfortunately, that you were born a Hivite. As such you are on the "hit list" of the approaching barbarians. That hit list includes the Hittites, Gergashites, Amorites, Canaanites, Perizzites, Hivites, and Jebusites. All of these people are to be wiped out, killed, massacred, annihilated or exterminated. Your spies confirm that it is the barbarians intention to put all men, women, boys, girls and infants to the sword. They want your land. Further these barbarians claim to have a very powerful god on their side, a god "whose sword will devour flesh, whose arrows are drunk with blood" [Deuteronomy 32:42], a god that will enable "two of their men to put to rout 10,000" [Deuteronomy 32:30] of ours. That god is, of course, our Christian god. How shall you, a Hivite, understand the injunction "Love your enemies?" We are to believe that Christ's father gave the command and personally assisted the barbarians in their annihilation of the seven tribes occupying the land the barbarians so hotly coveted. And now in the New Testament, Christ tells us that we should love our enemy? How shall you, a Hivite, love the enemy who has come to steal your land and to kill you, your wife and your children? The life sustaining reward of a land flowing with milk and honey does appear to go to those who annihilate their enemies, who then claim their dead enemies land as their own. This has been the repeated pattern of the colonial

European powers. Enemies were partially or wholly exterminated, and the ownership of the land changed hands. Their land became out land. And we Christians sermonized our colonial victims that your should "Love your enemy!?"

How shall a 20th century killing field victim "love his enemy" – a heartless, soulless sadistic monster, who on his next cigarette break will saunter over and blow your friend's brains out, only to remind you that it will soon be your turn?

Let us address the question to the President of the United States. Mr. G. Bush has stated that the 9/11 terrorists have declared war on the U.S. Those terrorists are the enemy of the U. S. Will we love our enemies? Or will we "hunt them down to the farthest corners of the earth" and kill them all to the best of our ability? The television evangelist Pat Robertson (September 2005) recommended publicly that the U. S. ought to "take out" Hugo Chavez, President of Venezuela, for his vitriolic anti U. S. statements. How can we understand Robertson's and Bush's willingness to kill enemies? Both are reported as being "born again Christians". Our options include:

a) Both are capable of saying "Yes, we love our enemies and yes we will kill our enemies" and no question, let alone the stress of a cognitive dissonance, pops into their minds.

b) Neither of them is aware of Christ's injunction to "love your enemy".

c) Both are fully aware of Christ's injunction to "love your enemy" and both have relegated that rule into the category of discardible insanity.

25) "Then I looked and on Mount Zion stood the lamb and with him were a hundred and forty four thousand who had his name and the name of the father written on their foreheads. ... That song no one could learn except the 144,000 who alone from the world had been ransomed. These are men who did not defile themselves with women, for they have kept themselves chaste." [Revelations 14:1-5] These are the 144,000 composed of 12,000 from each of the 12 tribes of Israel. They alone have been ransomed!? What about the billions of others? Only 12,000 from each of the 12 tribes? What about Russians and Japanese and Aztecs? But the greatest affront will arise from the total exclusion of all women. Gender discrimination? And all men who "defiled" themselves with women are also totally excluded? The holy sacrament of wedlock is insufficient to counter the inherent sin of sex? Are we to believe that sex within sanctified marriage still "defiles"? Only chaste virgin men!? It is too much. It also is utterly unacceptable. It joins the list of biblical quotations that our present sense of morality and justice simply cannot accept. It too will join the list of

effectively expunged quotations.

26) "The Lord has blinded the eyes of the people and he has made the people stubborn. He did this so that they could not see or understand and so that they would not turn to the Lord and be healed." [John 12:40]

This passage speaks loudly and plainly and denies everything that our present popular Christianity stands for. It too is effectively gone.

# Chapter 7
# Jesus Christ: Who Is He?

## Who is He?

There are a multitude of books available on this topic. It is, in a sense, a credit to the literary skill of C. S. Lewis to have narrowed the focus of this question. We know that C.S. Lewis is the resident philosopher/ logician/theologian for western Protestant Christianity. Even among Catholics, many draw intellectual certainty and comfort from the many books and essays that have issued from the mind of this man. Let there be no doubt whatever: in C. S. Lewis, Christians found a highly intelligent man who could be trusted to come to their aid. When boxed in by those repugnant sceptics and atheists, C. S. Lewis became their superman who could easily find wiggle room and then an escape route for the intellectually beleaguered Christian. We will notice a tendency among those Christians to accept uncritically the abstruse argumentations of their intellectual giant and hero. It was the conclusions reached by C. S. Lewis that were important: The bible, God, the prophets, Jesus Christ and the final heaven and hell. All these were proven to be authentic and real by the imponderable and abstruse logic of C. S. Lewis: If the quality of his logic was ever in doubt, his conclusions were never in doubt. They were so desperately sought that both his conclusions and his logic were raised to the level of unassailable truth. We have previously noted the possibility of an "anti-Eureka" moment for C. S. Lewis in connection with his "proof" that God cannot intervene miraculously in his suffering world. Should you be interested in the philosophical meanderings of this man, I highly recommend the books Christian Reflections and The Problem of Pain both, of course, by C. S. Lewis.

In his book, Christian Reflections, C. S. Lewis makes profound indirect statements about himself. He pursues the arcane topic of whether "human thought could be set aside as irrelevant to the real universe." He goes on to state "I now claim to have found the answer" [p63]. There is no recognition that new information may shed new light on the question. As with armchair logician/philosophers of the past he arrogates to himself the privilege of absolute certainty. Thus, C. S. Lewis can state: "We find that matter always obeys the same laws which our logic obeys. When logic says, a thing must be so, nature always agrees." [p64] And who is the prime logician of the 20th century? Of course it is C. S. Lewis himself. Can we detect some hubris here? Was C. S. Lewis so full of himself that he could actually make the statement "When logic says a thing must be so, nature always agrees?" Let us test that statement. What are some of the things that logic has said "must be so".

1) The Ptolemaic solar system, earth at the centre, the sun and the moon circling around.

2) Aristotelian physics, with no scientific verification desired or even permissible: Does not everyone know that heavy objects accelerate faster than light ones, under the force of gravity? Sorry, it is not so!

3) The witch trials with the logician/theologians presiding, determining that since the woman weighed more than the bible, she must, ipso facto, be a witch. Did anyone ever dare to test the validity of their logic? Did anyone recommend that the fat bishop should get on the scale?

4) With Galileo before the Holy Inquisition, we see a modern scientist who dared to say "your logic says 'it must be so' but my tests and verification show that your logic is erroneous." The logicians/ theologians/Inquisitors/Executors, of course, had their way. Where logic comes with the force of hangings, beheadings and burnings, logic is always right.

And yet mankind did make it through the Dark Ages. But C. S. Lewis in no way allowed or appreciated the fact that it was these armchair logicians who solved "all" relevant questions, with absolute certainty - it was those logicians that locked mankind into a mind fix with death penalties all around for those who would dare to tamper with these fixed certainties. The progress of mankind means: 1) an end to the Inquisition; 2) an end to witch trails; 3) an end to power of the Holy Roman Catholic Church, and subsequently the power of any church; 4) an end to suppression of scientific work, from dissection of cadavers to the germ theory of disease to stem cell research; 5) an end to slavery; 6) an end to government by kings, feudal lords or aristocrats, that is by a privileged caste. This short listing of what the progress of mankind means will clearly illustrate the cost or the active ingredient that will allow that progress to happen. The logicians, with their absolute certainty, must be disempowered and alternatively, the scientists from Galileo to Koch to Newton to Watt to Salk, these humble scientists must be viewed as the real benefactors of society. It is the contribution of the scientists that makes the jumbo A380 fly, that makes our cellphone work, that allows us to remove a clouded lens (cataract) to replace it with a clear lens, that allows hope for a vaccine against AIDS to be developed.

Of course our scientists use logic. But they use logic plus testing. And the Dark Ages represent logic, totally flawed logic, because it refused to allow the blessing brought in by the sceptic: lets devise a test to determine if our logic has some flaws hidden away inside it. The ultimate flaw of the logicians was the presumption of infallibility. It is in this area of testing logic, of considering the high likelihood of being wrong, together with a full measure of humility, that we find fault with the mountainous hubris of C. S. Lewis.

In answer to the question "Who was Christ?" C. S. Lewis offered the following answer: "Either he was a raving lunatic of an unusually abominable type or else he was, and is, precisely what he said." [The Problem of Pain, p12] Stated in such a categorical manner, in such a harshly judgmental manner, we have no choice but to agree immediately with the "Christ was the son of God" alternative.

The word raving has clear meaning: loud, obnoxious and incoherent. The word lunatic is also clear: a person marked by lunacy or insanity, affected by the cycles of the moon (luna). The word abominable is the most hurtful. If we presently encounter insanity, or mental disease, the word abominable would never be used to describe any person so afflicted. Abominable means worthy of extreme disgust, hatred, abhorrence, detestation and loathing. [Websters New Collegiate Dictionary] It means to detest in the highest degree. There is a clear connotation of moral repugnance. How can Lewis pass that kind of judgment on anyone whose mind may be diseased? Instead of sympathy, understanding and perhaps a quest for possible healing, Lewis heaps on the abuse of terming Christ's postulated lunacy as being unusually abominable.

We have made our choice if confronted with Lewis's two alternatives. But we see hidden in Lewis's two alternatives a challenge: can the case be made that Christ did suffer from some arcane form of mental disorder? We will leave a tentative diagnosis to an expert in psychology or psychiatry. What we will do is journey through the four gospels taking note of those actions and statements by Christ that may indicate that he suffered from mental disorders that are not unusually abominable, that are cause for sympathy. Let him who is without any mental disorders be the first to cast abominations!

Christ was born of the Virgin Mary. While she was engaged to Joseph, a Judean Israelite, she was visited by an angel, Gabriel, sent by God: "you are truly blessed! The Lord is with you. … The Lord God will make him king as his ancestor David was. He will rule the people of Israel forever and his kingdom will never end." [Luke 1:30-33] It is distressing to read these erroneous predictions, made by an angle sent by God, even before Christ was born. Christ did not become the consummate military leader that David was. Christ in no way even resembled David, who counted out 200 foreskins from killed Philistines to gain the hand in marriage of the king's (Saul's) daughter. [1 Samuel 18:25-27] He certainly did not rule the people of Israel forever. One wonders if Christ himself had the burden of these fantastic predictions loaded upon his mind. We do not know.

Matthew reports that Christ initiated his work by starting to preach, by quoting the words of John the Baptist: "Repent, for the kingdom of heaven is upon you." [Matthew 3:2 and Matthew 4:17] Christ quickly became famous. A man possessed by an evil spirit vaults Christ into immediate celebrity status. The possessed man shrieks, "Jesus of Nazareth, what do you want with us? Have you come to destroy us? I know who you are! You are the Holy One of God!" [Mark 1:24] What a dramatic way to announce Christ's identity. But to see that possessed man serve that purpose for Christ will awaken the sceptic in all of us. Do we have here an example of an evil spirit so burdened with a low IQ that "it" does Christ's bidding in correctly identifying Christ to all attending people, without forcing Christ to announce it himself? Can you imagine the confusion that the Prince of Deception would have created if his servant demon had identified Christ as Beelzebub's buddy? Or have him shout loudly "Of course I will do your bidding because I know that you are Lucifer's ally." Two chapters further we read of more evil spirits exorcised. But here the nonsensical order is given by Christ to the evicted evil spirits, "Jesus warned the spirits not to tell who he was" [Mark 3:12] And this order is given after the evil spirits had just been evicted and had just shouted for all to hear 'you are the Son of God'." [Mark 3:11] Do we have here an example of the alliance of evil, under Satan's direction, divided against itself? Or do we have an indication that this was a staged event, a deception that instantly produced faith and followers?

We know that the television evangelists with their frequent displays of miracles cannot pass the tests of authenticity that the sceptics have ready for them. We tend to feel that deception should never be used in persuading people of the merits or demerits of any cause. But it is not and has not always been regarded as categorically wrong. Firstly, if a minor wrong is utilized to achieve a major right, many will agree that the end does indeed justify the means. A bitter pill to achieve healing. Murder a tyrant to save his intended victims. Secondly, it is well known that people can be deceived so easily and effectively. Many people desire intensely to be given acceptable reasons (deception) in order to be able to retain highly cherished illusions. When war propagandists hold forth before their audiences the cherished illusion is military skill, boundless courage, and moral rectitude among "our boys". And for our enemies our desired illusion is that they are all evil animals that deserve to be killed. The deceptions go down like a cool beer on a hot summer afternoon. Politicians make it a compulsory duty to know what any particular audience wishes to hear. Election rhetoric comes to pass. Deceptions, and preferably half truths, become the order of the day. When doctors recognize a horrific disease in a patient, they must face a difficult question. Shall they give the patient the unadorned truth and risk having the patient slide into a resigned to die depression? Or should they sugar coat the truth to improve the patients morale, to leave the patient ready to take on the now seemingly beatable foe? If the deception is known to improve the survival rate of the patient, does deception stay wrong or is it the right way to go?

The television evangelists face a difficult question: deceive and succeed or integrity and boredom and failure? The audience will desire and expect miracles on the basis of previous miracle experiences and of course, on the basis of Christ's record himself: a miracle healer. We have noted previously the many miraculous signs, wonders and healings that Christ was credited with. So it needs to be expected that the modern evangelist, empowered by the Holy Spirit and by the empowering promises will be expected to perform miracles. Shouting and sweating, he/she will attempt to validate the cherished illusions of the audience. Sceptics will not be welcome. Should we verify that this person was fully deaf and now can hear normally? Shall we remind the audience that this believer has had his deafness cured five times already at previous miracle sessions? Shall we verify that the evangelist knows by cunning electronic means what ails this particular believer instead of the deception that the information came to the evangelist by miraculous means? We know that sceptics are as unwelcome to any present day evangelist as were the "wise and learned", the Teachers and Pharisees and Rabbis, to Christ in his day. Christ called them snakes and vipers and sons of Satan. He expressed joy that God had "hidden all this from the wise and educated." [Luke 10:21] It is highly damaging when an evangelist is caught "red-handed" in a blatant deception. Thus they will prefer to work "miracles" where the lines are blurred between a genuine miracle and a non-miraculous temporary sense of well being. Christ's loathing of the sceptics is thus very understandable. Surrounded by faithful, childlike and gullible believers his staged deceptions come off as fully genuine miracles. But with sceptics around him, Christ was effectively debilitated. The report in Mark states clearly that when surrounded by unbelieving sceptics in his hometown "Jesus could not work any miracles there." [Mark 6:5] We will take special note of the words "could not" in the quotation. Do we have an indication that Christ is not all powerful? Is it clear that, with our modern evangelists and also with Christ, when the sceptics are present to point out deceptions, miracles cannot be performed? When the sceptics are gone the situation is radically different.

On the assumption then, that Christ "could not" work miracles in the presence of sceptics, but that he did work miraculous deceptions when the sceptics were not present, what can we say about the mental state of Christ? The fact that Christ utilized deceptions sets Christ in the company of the vast majority of leaders in this world. His mental state thus far is perfectly normal and healthy.

Christ was convinced that the end of times was to happen very soon. Thus there was a great urgency to repent immediately. Sinning had to stop in order to go to heaven and avoid going to hell. In the context of this urgency Christ stated "If your hand causes you to sin cut it off … if your foot causes you to sin, chop it off … if your eye causes you to sin, poke it out." [Mark 9:43-47 and Matthew 18:8-9 and Matthew 5:29-30] Self mutilation advocated by Christ!? Self flagellation was a widely prescribed and utilized strategy within many Christian faiths to mortify the flesh, to resist the temptations of the flesh. Perhaps ones desire for sexual gratification or for other sinful gratifications would be diminished by scourging ones back until it is literally a bloody, painful mess. We know that, even presently, self flagellation among Muslim young men does happen and when infections set in, death can result. But here we go way beyond self flagellation. A scourging of the back will heal, and the scars will be seen as a badge of honour. But self mutilation? Where young men do this with the aim of avoiding conscription into the army, many western countries impose the death penalty. If my eye beholds an irresistibly beautiful woman, is the eye at fault or is it the "main frame computer"? Is it sufficient to "poke out and throw away" the right eyen when the left eye is still there to behold yet another ravishing woman? Here we are left with the depressing thought that just maybe Christ's mental state has slipped into a less than normal state. In our homes for the insane, or preferably, the mentally disturbed, we can find any number of patients who seem to have a deep and persistent desire to self mutilate. We try to prevent them from doing so. Is there any record in the Old Testament of a recommendation to self mutilate to avoid sinning? No. The Jewish point of view is very clear. Any self mutilation is always wrong.

"But I tell you to love your enemies and be good to everyone who hates you." [Luke 6:27 and Matthew 5:44] Here one wonders if Christ was fully aware of how iconoclastic his injunction was and is. Surely Jesus was aware of the warrior leader Joshua, and David and … . Surely he was aware of the warrior descriptions of Jehovah in the Old Testament. Was Joshua commanded by God to love the seven tribes inhabiting the promised land, or was he to annihilate and massacre all men, women and children to make way for the new vanquishing, blood drenched warriors? And after laying claim to the land of the defeated peoples, the new owners had to defend their claim by force of arms or lose it to new claimants. Loving your enemies is the equivalent of laying down and destroying your weapons. History provides a 99.9% guarantee that, upon your declaration of love for your enemies, or indeed, just a perceived weakening of your defenses, the enemy will be there pillaging, raping, enslaving and killing. Why only 99.9%?

After the horrific experience of the Second World War, the writer, Farley Mowat, had a compulsive yearning to meet a peoples totally devoid of the instinctive capacity for warfare. He went to far northern Canadian Territories. He met the peace loving Eskimos. And he also discovered why they could be so peace-loving and defenseless: their land was not considered desirable by anyone else. On rare occasions northern forest dwellers, the Indians, would follow herds of caribou into the "barrens" where they found the Eskimos. Massacres ensued. With the heart rendering scream of "Itkillet" [the Indians are coming] all Eskimos would race into the barrens hoping that, thereby, not all would fall victim to the Indians. [The People of the Deer. Farley Mowat]

Even at this point, we are far from loving our enemy. We do realize that war with our holocaustic weaponry is unacceptable, and we recognize that we must co-exist with our enemies. But we do not love our enemies. Thus we have another small question mark raised over Christ's mental state. Perhaps he was an idealist many millennia ahead of his time. And then again maybe his mind had again slipped into territory no longer fully in touch with reality.

In Matthew we read Christ's instructions to the twelve apostles. "Do not take the road to the Gentile lands, do not enter any Samaritan town, go only to the lost sheep of the house of Israel." [Matthew 10:5-7] We have noted earlier that these instructions specifically exclude Gentiles and Samaritans. And this command not to go to certain peoples is followed up by the statement "Go only to the people of Israel." And this is followed up by Christ's extreme sense of urgency: the date of his coming with his kingdom was to happen in the very near future. "I tell you this: before you have gone through all the towns of Israel, the Son of Man will have come." [Matthew 10:23]

Thus we have a very unsettling picture. The apostles are to carry their saving message only to the Israelites. Gentiles and Samaritans - be damned - literally. And even before all of Israel has been covered in this hurried saving message blitz, the end will be ushered in. Does this exclusion of Gentiles and Samaritans reflect on Christ's mental state in any negative way? Not at all. Jesus' theological certainties included the primary one that characterizes all of the Old Testament and most of the New Testament: the Israelites were the people chosen by God to be his people. In Christ's mind the hardening of Pharaoh's heart and the consequent plagues and the killing of all first borns among all Egyptians made sense. The Israelites were the privileged and favored people. The Egyptians were <u>not</u> privileged and <u>not</u> favored. Now, in the context of Christ's instructions to his apostles, we see a substitution: the Egyptians have been replaced by the Gentiles. We have tended to accept the horrific treatment of the Egyptians without any serious thought or misgiving. Sunday school treatment of Exodus left us, the kids, with a palpable hatred for the "evil" Pharaoh. It is much more difficult to accept when <u>we</u> are to be given the Egyptians status.. Just as there never was any intention to bring Egyptians to salvation, we now see that there is no intention to bring us, the Gentiles, to salvation: "Stay away from the Gentiles." We have read before "All Egypt will send up a great cry of anguish … but among all Israel not a dog's tongue shall be so much as scratched." [Exodus 11:6-7] How little sense of injustice was aroused. No alarm bells went off. Now if we substitute ourselves, the Gentiles for the Egyptians, the flavour changes dramatically. The full weight of the favouritism, the chosen versus the rejected, settles in on our minds. But, this then, while it may cause us distress, in no way reflects negatively on Christ's mental state. It was perfectly normal and healthy Israelite thinking.

In Matthew, Jesus states "When people want to borrow money, loan it to them." [Matthew 5:42] In Luke he goes much further: "If you lend money only to those that you think will pay you back, will God be pleased with you for that? Even sinners lend to sinners because they think they will get it all back. … Lend without expecting to be paid back." [Luke 6:34-35] We do not expect Christ to be a PhD level economist. But we do expect a level of common sense that this directive from Christ does not satisfy. It is clear at even a common sense level that if people borrow money, aware that no action will be taken if they default, many will default. And others who should not borrow at all will throw all caution to the wind and borrow the absolute maximum. Lending money with no expectation to be repaid becomes something quite different from a loan. It becomes a charitable donation, or indeed, it becomes a form of theft with no retaliation. There would be a tendency for people to view the capital proceeds from such loans with the adage: easy come - easy go. It would result in wasted money. It would also very quickly result in all available funds for loans being exhausted. There would be a rush to borrow as much money as possible followed up by the creditors realization that they now have no more funds left for loan purposes. Does Christ's directive indicate mental disorder? Perhaps he should not have ventured into the area of economics. Perhaps he did not think through what he was advocating. But we see here very little evidence of mental imbalance.

"When Jesus ... left Bethany the next morning, he was hungry. Observing a fig tree some distance off, covered with foliage, he went over to see if he could find anything on it. When he reached it, he found nothing but leaves; it was not the time (season) for figs. Then addressing it he said, 'Never again shall anyone eat of your fruit.' His disciples heard all this ... the next morning they saw the fig tree withered to its roots. Peter remembered and said to him, "Rabbi, look! The fig tree you cursed has withered up.' In reply Jesus told them, 'Put your trust in God. I solemnly assure you, whoever says to this mountain 'Be lifted up and thrown into the sea and has no inner doubts, but believes what he says will happen, shall have it done for him. I give you my word if you are ready to believe, that you will receive whatever you ask for in prayer'." [New American Bible. St. Anthony Guild Edition. Mark 11:12-25] This is deeply distressing. He tells his disciples "whatever you ask for, you will receive" and only twenty four hours earlier the Son of God himself approaches a fig tree, searches for figs, finds none because it is out of season and becomes sufficiently incensed that an utterly unbelievable spectacle results. He stands before the tree, looks at it and "addresses" it. In the opinion of his disciples, he curses it. We may have seen a young child searching in vain for strawberries in the patch - it is too early -there are only flowers. Anger at the strawberry plants? Or we may have seen an intoxicated hobo looking for cherries on a tree with the season long over. Anger at the cherry tree? Anger at any tree at any time? For those of us that have any ties to the care of fields, gardens or orchards, the spectacle of Christ "losing it" at a tree with no figs because it is out of season, leaves no doubt whatever. That man has taken leave of his senses. And to see and hear him then go on to "solemnly assure" his disciples that they can tell this mountain "be lifted up and thrown into the sea" only confirms and validates the prior diagnosis Move mountains - no problem! Put some fruit on a fig tree - big problem! Now we do indeed have a mental aberation, not an unusually abominable problem, just a pitiful and pathetic problem. And this diagnosis only tackles the problem from the

"Son of Man" side.

From the "Son of God" side the problems are insurmountable. The all-knowing Son of God is presented as everything but all-knowing. He does not even know if the foliage bearing fig tree actually has figs on it. He must go over and spread out the leaves to see if he could find any figs. He does not know the season for figs! He who was there when the fig tree was created, he who, according to the Trinity, created the fig tree, and, he who previously judged all of his creations, including the fig tree, as being very good (Genesis), now shows that he doesn't even understand how his own creation functions. The fig tree has not changed but the evaluation of it changes from very good to very bad. Christ is enraged at the fig tree despite the fact that the fig tree is doing exactly what it was purposed to do when he created it. The top-up is the vehemence of his anger at his own creation and finally his curse to kill it. The Son of God claim seems very difficult to sustain.

In John we read of Jesus' brothers daring to admonish him. Why don't you go to Judea to the Festival of Shelters [Sukkoth, in Hebrew] where everyone can see what you are doing. "No one does anything in secret if they want others to know about them." [John 7:1-5] We have noted previously [Matthew 9:30-31, Mark 8:30, Luke 8:56, etc.] where on many occasions Christ admonished the faithful "not to tell anyone what had happened." Was this just a "clever" strategy to maximize the proliferation of his salvation message? Or, are "clever" strategies always wrong in broadcasting Christ's message? We do know that Christ did not appreciate the advice from his brothers. Repeating the expression twice that "my time has not yet come," he informs them that he would not go to Judea, to the Festival of Shelters. "I am not going." [John 7:8] Then we encounter a reversal in Christ's thinking. At the wedding at Cana, Christ said, "Woman, your concerns are not my concerns, my time has not yet come." And ten minutes later that statement is effectively reversed and becomes, "Yes woman, your concerns are my concerns, and my time has come" and the water to wine miracle is completed. In a much more direct way, we now have a similar reversal. "After Jesus' brothers had gone to the festival, he decided to go and he went secretly." [John 7:10] Thus we see the statement "I am not going" changed to "I will go secretly." On the Son of Man level we have merely a change of mind. On the Son Of God level, the problems are again insurmountable. An all-knowing God is never allowed the privilege of a change of mind because there can be no such thing as unexpected new information. With respect to Christ's mental state, it indicates little more than a degree of uncertainty about what course of action to follow.

We have noted that Christ had an extreme sense of urgency about his message. Very little time was left before he would return with his kingdom. And the date of that return would be like the chief examiners instructions about the end of the allotted time to university students in the examination halls. "Your time is over. Hand in your papers now." After that will come the evaluation or judgment - you will be informed of your pass or fail mark. Likewise you will be informed as to where you will go to spend eternity, heaven, or hell. Everyone was extremely interested to know the exact date of Christ's return. Christ made it clear, again, that he was not all-knowing. He stated "the Son himself doesn't know. Only the Father knows" [Mark 13:32] the exact date and time. But Christ remained extremely precise on what he did know: "I promise you that some of those standing here will not die before they see the Son of Man coming with his kingdom." [Matthew 16:28] Christ was so sure and emphatic about this that this statement is reiterated twice in Matthew [Matthew 24:34], again in Mark [Mark 13:30], in Luke [Luke 9:27 and 21:32] and in John where Jesus states to Peter with reference to Jesus favorite disciple, "What is it to you if I want him to live until I return?"

We have calculated earlier that if Christ's return was to happen before "all those standing here" will have died, the approximate maximum number of years to be spent waiting for Christ's return would be eighty years. Many more than eighty years have passed since Christ made the statement. All those then living are long long dead. We are faced with the fact that his apparently firm knowledge about the date of his return was in error.

Many people have illusions or delusions about a variety of things. If these things are of minor significance, no negative diagnosis of their mental state results. If these things are of major significance with life and death in the balance, with fortunes and poverty and health involved, we have no difficulty at all, in fact we are forced, to label them as delusional. Thus if we attach any major significance to the date of Christ's return, we will be forced to give a distressing diagnosis to Christ. He was in a delusional mental state. And there can be no doubt - the date of his return is of monumental significance. Here Christ shows himself to be much worse than not all-knowing. Here he was at a level of total certainty. And the test of its truth was to be answered, inexorably, by the mere passage of time. The time passed and we have the conclusion that Christ was delusional. What of God, Jesus' father? Would God allow his son certainties that were not correct? Thus the questions mount not just of Christ but also of God. It is a very distressing set of facts that we confront here.

Jesus died on a cross. And it is clear from the Holy Scriptures that he knew it was going to happen. It is equally clear that, whenever Jesus mentioned his coming death, the disciples did what they could to dissuade him from that course of action. "The nation's leaders, the chief priest, and the teachers ... will make the Son of Man suffer terribly. He will be rejected and killed but three days later he will rise to life. Then 'Jesus explained clearly what he meant.' " [Bible for Today's Family. Mark 8:31-32] It is extremely unfortunate that the writer of this gospel did not record what that explanation was. Because we are in desperate need of an explanation as to why it was necessary for Christ to die. Was it, in fact, a God imposed requirement for atonement to take place? Endless toil and pain can be endured if we have a very good reason for it. Even after Christ's "clear explanation" Peter was not at all satisfied with Christ's logic. "Peter took Jesus aside and told him to stop talking like that." [Mark 8:32] Other translations say Peter "remonstrated" or even "rebuked" Jesus for his plan to go to Jerusalem and die. Jesus reacts with great anger: "Satan get away from me!" It is a great shock to hear Christ calling Peter Satan. Other editions have Christ saying "Get out of my sight, you Satan." [New American Bible. Mark 8:33] Christ's mind was very firmly made up that he would go to Jerusalem, to suffer and to die. Thus we must conclude that he had an intense death wish. And his "clear explanation" to his disciples in no way satisfied the disciples. Significantly Peter says, "Lord, surely God won't let this happen to you!" What kind of explanation did Christ give if Peter thinks that God opposes Jesus' plan to die, that indeed God "won't let it happen?" [Matthew 16:22]

Luke's record of these events is utterly contrary to Mark's impression. Instead of Christ speaking about his death "plainly" or indeed, "explaining clearly what he meant" we now have the words, " 'Pay close attention to what I am telling you! The Son of Man will be handed over to his enemies.' But the disciples did not know what he meant. The meaning was hidden from them. They could not understand it and they were afraid to ask." [Luke 9:44-45] What remains clear is the intense death wish on the part of Christ and the shock and sadness of his disciples. And the intense and angry response, on Christ's part against Peter, who clearly opposed Christ's plan.

How can we understand Christ's death wish? Our present, most popular atonement theory holds that Christ had to die to provide "satisfaction" to God, to open the door to the possibility of salvation. Perhaps that was the non-recorded "clear explanation". But it was not recorded. Whatever explanation was or was not given, the disciples were saddened and horrified by the prospect. We are given the spectacle of Peter being called Satan for opposing Christ's death plan while Satan does everything in his power to support Christ's death plan. Our theological understanding of what is going on is in tatters. Should Peter have aligned himself with Satan in support of Christ's death plan?

"But three days later he will rise to life." What is left of Christianity (for most Christians) without the miracle of the Resurrection? We are not allowed any doubt on this concept. But how can we avoid thinking wasn't Christ just as convinced that he would return with his kingdom "before all of you presently standing around me have died." This absolute certainty of Christ was proven, by the passage of time, to be wrong. Now we have the absolute certainty that "three days later I will rise to life." We have previously studied the biblical record of Christ's resurrection. The many contradictions, the disguises that left Christ unrecognizable to his very closest associates, these don't help us at all.

But here it is the death wish that troubles us the most. When people are grievously ill with a progressive, debilitating, painful disease, most of us can sympathize with and experience deep empathic understanding for that victim when the death wish arises. Bring an end to this misery. Heal the disease if we can, but if that option is fully impossible, we will exercise the Shakespearean option "life lacks not the power to dismiss itself." And where that life does lack that power, or where life lacks the power to bring about a relatively dignified death, we hope that friends, genuine friends, can be found to help bring about that death. Death can indeed terminate misery. But where there is no misery to be terminated, the death wish is indeed a sure sign of a mental disturbance. Christ was at the apex of his productive life. Any thought to actively contribute to a sequence of events culminating in death violates any concept of sanity.

Thus we do have questions about Christ's mental state. We have seen his instruction to self mutilate and to love enemies. We are aware of his delusional certainty with respect to his date of return. His death wish has left us, as well as the disciples, shocked and saddened. A lunatic subject to insane mood swings under the power of the moon? We think not. Raving lunatic? Strong opinions, yes. Raving? We think not. Unusually abominable? To think of people suffering from mental disorders as being "unusually abominable" is in fact unusually abominable. On the first option provided by C. S. Lewis, we find ourselves in vehement disagreement.

His second option is that Christ was God incarnate, in the form of the Son of God. We have seen repeatedly that Christ was not all-knowing. We think of the fig tree spectacle. We think of his statement that "I don't know the exact date and time." We have seen that Christ was not all-powerful. We remember the statement that "he could not" work miracles in the presence of faithless sceptics. Finally, we know that Christ continued the Israelite heritage of the chosen People. It is impossible for us to consider Christ benevolent when his instructions read "Do not go to the Gentiles." The second option provided by C. S. Lewis fails just as badly as the first option. We are forced to recognize that the great logician had it all wrong.

Who was Christ now becomes a much more complicated question because Christ was a very complicated man. We are not really sure of his ancestry, but prefer to believe that the entire gospel of John has it right: Joseph and Mary were his genetic parents. When he actually arrives on the scene at approximately thirty years of age, we see a powerful charisma together with prophetic ambitions. And an intense loathing for the book smart, ethically challenged religious leaders of his day. And his anger knew no bounds when these leaders, the learned and the wise, demanded a miracle that he knew he couldn't deliver. His appeal was to the people, not the aristocratic or theological leadership. His opposition to those in power lead us to detect in him a bias in favor of empowering the people. Imagine him talking to women! Never did he embrace the Old Testament style death penalty. And his primary message: love one-another. His love and concern did not extend to Gentiles. But we ought to have an easy time forgiving that lack. Is it not grossly unfair to expect any person to make a moral quantum leap forward? Actual improvements tend to come in tiny increments. So what Christ did represents, in many ways, that which it was possible to do. Further we recognize that those who undertake to attack, challenge and change the established order must be possessed of zeal, idealism, charisma, and last, but not least, some delusions. You must speak with authority and unlimited certainty. Only time will tell us which of those delusions were challenges which could and would be overcome and which of those delusions were, in fact, delusions. It is not easy to know the difference. It is easy to see that his primary message, to love one-another, is a wonderful message. And we have no difficulty extending that message, for Jesus, to the Gentiles as well.

# BIBLIOGRAPHY

The New English Bible, with Apocrypha, Oxford University Press, 1970.
The New American Bible, Catholic Biblical Association of America, St. Anthony Guild Press Patterson, New Jersey, 1970.
Bible for Today's Family, American Bible Society, New York, 1970.
New Jerusalem Bible, Readers Edition, New York, 1990.
Holy Bible K.J.V. Amplified, Parallel Bible, Zondervan Corporation, Grand Rapids, Michigan, 1987.
The Book. Tyndale House Publishers, Wheaton, Illinois, 1984.
The Biblical Doctrine Of The Atonement, John Scott Lidgett, Klock and Klock Christian Publishers, Minneapolis, Minnesota, 1983. ISBN 086524-145-7
The Atonement of the Death of Christ, H.D. McDonald, Baker Book House, Grand Rapids, Michigan. ISBN 0-8010-6194-6
Suffering and God, A. E. McGrath, Zondervan Publishing House, 1995. ISBN 0-310-40691-9
The Problem of Pain, C. S. Lewis, Collins Clear-Type Press, 1940.
Why Do People Suffer?, James Jones, Lion Publishing. ISBN 0-7459-2419-0
Where is God When it Hurts?, Philip Yancey, Zondervan Corporation. ISBN 0-310-35410-2
Christian Reflections, C. S. Lewis, W. B. Eerdmans Publishing Company, Grand Rapids, Michigan.
Mere Christianity, C. S. Lewis. ISBN 0-06-065292-6
The DaVinci Code, Dan Brown, Doubleday, 2003.
Peace is the Way, Deepak Chopra, Harmony Books, 2005.
Judaism and Christianity, the Differences, Trude Weiss-Rosmarin, Jonathon David Publishers Inc., Middle Village, New York, 1997.
The Purpose Driven Life, Rick Warren, Zondervan, 2002.
How Good Do We Have To Be?, Harold S. Kushner, Little, Brown and Company, 1996.
The Trial and Death of Jesus, Haim Cohn, Harper Collins Publishers, Konecky and Konecky, 1963.
A New Christianity for a New World, J. S. Spong, Harper, San Francisco, 2002.
Kepler's Witch, James A. Connor, Harper Collins Publishers, 2005.

www.ingramcontent.com/pod-product-compliance
Ingram Content Group UK Ltd.
Pitfield, Milton Keynes, MK11 3LW, UK
UKHW041944190726
13854UKWH00004B/1790

9 781412 097598